SALES
TALK

SALES TALK

HOW TO POWER UP SALES THROUGH VERBAL MASTERY

BY LEN SERAFINO

ADAMS MEDIA CORPORATION
Avon, Massachusetts

Published by Adams Media, an F+W Publications Company
57 Littlefield Street, Avon, MA 02322 U.S.A.
www.adamsmedia.com

ISBN: 1-58062-851-6

Printed in Canada.

J I H G F E D C

Library of Congress Cataloging-in-Publication Data
Serafino, Len.
Sales talk / Len Serafino.
p.   cm.
ISBN 1-58062-851-6
1. Sales presentations. 2. Selling. I. Title.

HF5438.8.P74 S47 2003
658.85--dc21
                                    2002153896

This publication is designed to provide accurate and authoritative information with regard to the subject matter covered. It is sold with the understanding that the publisher is not engaged in rendering legal, accounting, or other professional advice. If legal advice or other expert assistance is required, the services of a competent professional person should be sought.
—From a *Declaration of Principles* jointly adopted by a Committee of the American Bar Association and a Committee of Publishers and Associations

Many of the designations used by manufacturers and sellers to distinguish their products are claimed as trademarks. Where those designations appear in this book and Adams Media was aware of a trademark claim, the designations have been printed with initial capital letters.

This book is available at quantity discounts for bulk purchases.
For information, call 1-800-872-5627.

For Nancy Karen

Acknowledgments

Writing is a solitary act. It's impossible to write without being comfortable with being alone for long stretches. Yet, I could never have completed this book without the incredible amount of help, support, and constructive criticism I received along the way. When I started to tell people I was writing a book on sales, one of the most gratifying discoveries for me was the unqualified enthusiasm they expressed. Friends and business associates alike offered to help with the project.

I want to thank John Anderson, CEO of MRI Nashville for reading, editing, and above all challenging me to make needed improvements. He believed I could do it. It helped more than I can say, John. Thank you as well to Brenda Albright, an educator with extraordinary communication skills. Her insights and creativity were critical to keeping me focused on the communication aspect of selling.

I am blessed to have a number of friends who agreed to read *Sales Talk* and offer comments. I am indebted to Joanne Mayfield of AccuImage, Deanna Osborn, and Richard Worthen of Medical Specialties Inc.

Many others offered anecdotes and insights, answered questions, and suggested new topics for exploration. I want to personally thank Don Abramo of Eckert Drug, Inc., Barbara Butler, Don Carlberg of West Corporation, Elaine del Rossi of HTH Worldwide, Bonnie Douglas of ResMed, Johnny Drake of Puritan Bennett, Roger Fenlon, Sandy Ferrin of Upstate Homecare, Blair Johnston of Respironics Inc., Linda Kilpatrick, Dennis Nelson, Bob Renga of Acton Medical Associates,

Audrey Riffenberg of Riffenberg Associates, C. Frank Riley of South Georgia Health Partners, Rick Shore of Respironics Inc., and my good friend Al Shredagavis.

I must say a special word of thanks to Adams Media, especially publishing director Gary Krebs, who pushed me to finish the book, and my editor, Danielle Chiotti, whose insights and patient persistence made *Sales Talk* a better book.

To my colleagues at American HomePatient, thank you for giving me the opportunity to be part of a courageous team.

Finally, thank you to my parents for making sure I got an education, to my wife, Nancy, whose constant encouragement and support kept me going, and to my children, Jeremy and Kristi, you're the best.

Contents

CONTENTS

Introduction

Sales Talk is a book that will show you how you can increase sales results by improving your communications skills. Let's consider for a moment the four key attributes of a successful salesperson.

1. *An outgoing personality.* People with outgoing personalities are often told they could make it big in sales. If you like to talk, if you're quick with a joke, and if you're happiest when surrounded by other people, sales can be a wonderful career choice. At least that's the traditional view of the salesperson. While perhaps still true, it isn't enough today.

2. *Persistence.* A successful salesperson has to be resilient to survive. Salespeople hear the word *no* a lot. Sometimes the buyer means it. More often than most of us realize, however, buyers want to buy, but they need a reason or justification for their purchase. It's your job to help them find good reasons to buy.

3. *Product knowledge.* In simpler times a smile, friendly pats on the back, and a deaf ear to the word *no* might have made you enough sales to earn a good living. We live in a much more complicated world now. We are inundated with information every day. Rather than simplifying our lives, information adds complexity. As a result, specialization rules the day. There are doctors who specialize in neonatology and pediatric oncology, employment recruiters who specialize in industries and

even jobs within industries, and consultants who focus strictly on higher education. Customers need more help these days to make good decisions. As a result, product knowledge is more important than ever. Successful sales professionals have to be consultants to their customers, helping them make wise choices. In fact, product knowledge alone isn't enough. You have to understand your industry and the business principles that govern it. Trying to sell more products without understanding and addressing the customers' issues won't work anymore.

4. *Communication skills.* All the product knowledge in the world is useless if you can't communicate it to your customers in a way that helps them see the quality and value of your solution. In a complex world, customers have shorter attention spans. They have too little time and too much on their plates. You have to make every word count.

Most of us take communication for granted. After all, it's something we've been doing since we were born. From our first cry to let Mom know we were hungry to our most recent phone conversation, we all communicate. Yet, the ability to express our thoughts clearly and concisely is not a given; effective communication has to be learned.

Sales Talk is about recognizing the role communication plays in successful selling and putting that knowledge to work.

I have spent the better part of my career either selling or buying services. I worked for many years as a buyer, negotiating with health care providers who were eager to sell their services to my employer, the Blue Cross and Blue Shield Plans. I also spent ten years successfully selling services to health plans and physicians. More recently, I returned to the buyer's side of the table, responsible for purchasing medical equipment and software for a publicly traded home care company. I've had the good fortune to sit on both sides of the table. My experience has given me a unique perspective on sales.

Moreover, I am a longtime student of the art and science of communication. Extensive reading and a long-term affiliation with Toastmasters, an international organization dedicated to improving communication and leadership skills, has made me acutely aware of differences in communication styles. More important perhaps, I have seen the role communication skills play in whether a sale is made or lost. Many otherwise intelligent people consistently fail to communicate their ideas or desires effectively. Much of this failure can be attributed to a lack of preparation and planning. Most of us have the innate skills necessary to communicate effectively. However, it requires conscious thought and effort to tap these skills.

What makes communication skills so important to selling? We live in a communication-saturated society. Each day marketers expose Americans to 12 million display ads, 3 million radio ads, and more than 300,000 television commercials. Millions of e-mail messages are sent daily. People are constantly busy, and worse, they have more communication gadgets than ever to keep them occupied, and not just in the office with a phone, a fax, and a personal computer. We carry cell phones, Internet-enabled beepers, or personal digital assistants wherever we go. With all that competition, it's not easy to be heard and harder still to be understood. To reach your audience, you must keep it simple. With customers' shorter attention spans, it helps if you are entertaining, too.

It's natural to worry about the competition in terms of its product's features and benefits and its price. In some ways though, that is the easy part. Since we rarely, if ever, get to watch our competitors in action, most of us probably don't think much about how effective their presentations are. In other words, do they have better communication skills?

Here's some really important news. When it comes to presentation skills, you are competing not only with salespeople selling the same products but also with salespeople in other fields. If you are selling steel, believe it or not, on some level you are competing with your customer's paper products sales representative. Why? Your customers have only so much time. Naturally, they prefer to spend it with people whose company they enjoy. A buyer sees a lot of sales presentations. Listening to several presentations a day, buyers develop expectations, and ultimately preferences, based on the quality of the presentations.

Let me tell you a story that demonstrates the impact of being outflanked by a competitor as a result of differences in communication strategies. Not long ago, I set up meetings with two competing companies. The purpose of the meetings was identical. Each company was to present its newest medical equipment to our buying group.

Both companies had ideas about how they could help us sell more of their products to our customers, benefiting both organizations. Finding a convenient time for everyone on our staff proved to be a challenge. It turned out that the best solution required scheduling the meetings back to back. The first meeting ran from 1:00 P.M. to 4:00 P.M. The second meeting began with dinner that night at 6:00 and picked up again at 8:30 the following morning.

Within ten minutes of opening the one o'clock meeting, it was painfully obvious that Company *A* came in with no real plan. They were not well prepared. They didn't have enough copies of their handouts. Although their presentation begged for audiovisual aids, they had none. They brought only one piece of equipment. They didn't pass it around for us to touch. As they described their new marketing support programs, they continually apologized for the fact that they were only partly done.

Frankly, the energy level in the room was low. They had the look and feel of a company in the doldrums. As a longtime customer, we felt as if we were being taken for granted.

That evening, Company B took us to dinner. They reserved a private room, giving us an intimate environment that encouraged conversation. When we arrived in our conference room the next morning, they had five different pieces of equipment—several of them quite heavy—in place and waiting for us. They had arranged delivery late the afternoon before. Four different people presented. Each presentation was unique. The presenters used a combination of PowerPoint slides and videotape to enhance their message. They gave the PowerPoint presentations using a projector they'd brought with them. They gave us portfolios and pens sporting their logo and brought muffins to go with our coffee. The presenters were knowledgeable, candid, well organized, and enthusiastic. Overall, it was an excellent presentation.

Although the difference between their products was not substantial, Company B made Company A look like amateurs. Company A probably was more unlucky than bad. The contrast between the two was so stark that Company A's poor performance suffered all the more because of the immediacy of the comparison with Company B. Think about that the next time you visit one of your customers. Your presentation is being compared to others. Are you as prepared as you should be? You dare not take your customer for granted. Your competition won't.

One thing you won't get out of this book is a script that tells you exactly what to say in the various sales situations that arise. There are some examples, but don't assume that all you have to do is repeat the words I've written to achieve the desired result. In fact, you may disagree with my approach. That's fine. I hope you will consider carefully how you would communicate in the same situation. After all, that is the point of the book.

There will be times when you are forced to adjust your strategy right in the middle of a sales call. The question from left field, the objection you never heard before, a new complaint about service. Improving your communication skills will make it a lot easier to craft something on the spot that works. Your response may not be terrific the first time, but similar situations usually arise. By spending time thinking about how you can improve your response the next time, you'll improve it with every opportunity.

This book is not about sales techniques, meaning it isn't an alternative to Professional Selling Skills, SPIN Selling, consultative selling, relationship selling, or any of the myriad techniques that promise to increase your sales results. Although any of these techniques will work if put into practice effectively, *Sales Talk* focuses on identifying, building, and then using the communication skills you need to be an effective sales professional, *regardless* of the techniques you embrace.

I wrote this book because I am convinced that your communication skills are every bit as important as the products and services you sell. If you really want to enjoy a successful career in sales, you will have to learn to communicate effectively. *Sales Talk* will put you on the road to being an effective sales communicator.

Chapter 1

Becoming an Effective Communicator

First, Assess Your Communications Skills

When I turned thirty-five, I decided it was time to get regular exercise. I took regular walks and fiddled with a few dumbbells I had left over from school. By the time I was forty, I got serious and joined a health club. As I write this, I'm still working out three or four times a week. One morning when I was really struggling to get through my thirty minutes on the treadmill, it occurred to me that life would be a lot easier if exercise were like college.

In college, you study for four years, get a diploma, and you're done. Finished. No more term papers, no more exams. Just frame the certificate and move on. Wouldn't it be great if four years of workouts netted you a certificate and you could throw away your sweats forever?

Obviously, physical fitness doesn't work that way. Neither does learning. The fact is, building communication skills requires constant effort. Yet, like regular exercise, it can be done without taking up an inordinate amount of your time. Maybe you're already giving up an hour of television three times a week for exercise. Another thirty minutes a day, on average, is all you need to begin building your communication skills.

To get started, assess your skills now. Here are several ways to get some insights into your current strengths and weaknesses as a communicator:

- *Take a vocabulary test.* Most bookstores carry vocabulary books that contain tests along with self-scoring systems. Assessing your strengths and weaknesses will give you a good starting point. Remember, the more words in your vocabulary the more likely you can express yourself effectively.
- *Write down your strengths and weaknesses as a communicator.* Are you confident about your ability to communicate? In other words, do you consider yourself a good communicator, comfortable in any situation, or do you dread standing in front of a group? Are you able to hold the attention of others when you speak? Are you comfortable expressing your views in both business and social situations? If not, why not?
- *Ask family, friends, and coworkers you trust for their opinions of your strengths and weaknesses as a communicator.* Are you a good listener? Do they understand what you are saying most of the time? Do you tend to run on or overexplain? Can you disagree without being disagreeable? How people perceive you is critical to your success as a communicator. How do their observations compare to your list?

Although gathering this type of information is hardly a formal assessment of your abilities, it isn't a bad way to benchmark your skills and identify key areas that might need improvement.

In the next four segments we will discuss how reading, undertaking a vocabulary program, developing speaking skills, and becoming a keen observer can put you on the road to becoming a better communicator.

Everyone must row with the oars he has.

—English proverb

Read, Read, Read

Are you the type of person who is constantly looking for something to read? Consider yourself blessed if you like to read a good book. Better still if you're the one who always seems to have your nose in a book, a magazine, or the newspaper.

On the other hand, if reading isn't one of your favorite pastimes, you can learn to enjoy it, at least a little bit. Start by setting aside just fifteen minutes a day to read something.

How does reading help you develop communication skills? For one thing, reading exposes you to different writing styles, which are, after all, communication styles. A romance novel doesn't read like an article in the *Wall Street Journal*. Nor does a *Wall Street Journal* article read like a trade publication. Without even consciously trying, you will pick up clues that show you new ways to get your point across. Reading, especially if you like variety, also exposes you to new words, which in turn helps to build your vocabulary. The education you get from reading will come in handy when you need to make a key point in your sales presentation. The more interests you have, the more interesting you become to your client.

Let me give you an example. Say you want to persuade your customer to switch from brass fittings to aluminum. The customer is resistant. He's comfortable with the old way. You could just tell him he's out of step with the current trends. You could explain why your product is superior. But an analogy or story might get you where you want to go faster. In response to your customer's objection, you might use an analogy similar to the following one.

I see your point. It reminds me of a battle going on right now in the wine industry. People are used to real corks in their wine bot-

tles. But some winemakers are switching to plastic corks or screw caps because they are airtight, which greatly reduces the chances of spoilage.
Some people don't like it, though. Real cork is more romantic. Of course, once wine lovers realize that plastic will protect their investment in a good bottle of wi ne, their resistance will very likely disappear.

In this example, my interest in wine, and the knowledge I gained reading about it, provided an interesting way to make a point without simply telling the customer to get over it, or that times change, or that our product was superior to what they were using. Chances are you have a hobby or in-depth knowledge about a topic that can be a source of useful stories or analogies.

What kind of reading should you do? I firmly believe it is almost impossible to go wrong if your goal is to become more informed. Here are a few general suggestions.

Books

As a sales professional, you want to learn as much about your profession as possible. Read a book on selling skills at least once a year. Reading self-help books about speaking or writing is another great way to improve those skills. If you can't find something new to read this year, reread one you particularly liked from years past.

Reading books on subjects you find interesting is a marvelous way to continue your education. If you read just one book a month that's twelve a year. One hundred and twenty books in ten years. Reading at this rate amounts to about twelve pages a day—a modest goal. Yet, the payoff in terms of personal growth and knowledge is enormous.

Industry-Specific Trade Journals

Read your industry's trade journal to stay abreast of the latest trends. You'll know what the hot new ideas are and it will stimulate your own creativity. While you're reading the articles, don't ignore the advertisements. Print ads can tell you something about the way your competitors communicate with your customers and prospects. Take a look at the way companies you don't compete with talk to your customers, too. Are you sending the same message? Can you do better?

Business and Current Events Magazines

There's a wealth of information to be found in magazines like *BusinessWeek, Newsweek,* and *Time.* You certainly don't have to be an expert on every topic, but some familiarity with what is happening in the world will help you well beyond the time you invest in reading these magazines. When the conversation turns to the latest hot topic, be ready to make a contribution. Remember that every thing you say and do communicates something about you.

Imagine what kind of message you communicate when you say nothing at all?

Here are four tips that will keep you reading:

1. As soon as you get a periodical, skim through it, looking for interesting articles. Tear out the articles of interest and throw away the rest of the magazine. That's right, toss out the stuff you really don't want and won't read anyway. Then your pile won't get so big. It's easy to build an intimidating pile of reading material. Newspaper clippings, trade journal stories, and material you've downloaded from the Web can stack up in no time. In fact it can get so bad, it's easy to decide not to read any of it. Here's something you can do about it. When you have a few minutes between appointments

or maybe a two-hour flight, take your reading folder along, knowing it's filled with only the material you need.

2. When you decide to tackle something new, be patient with yourself. Initially, the subject matter might seem strange. It's easy to get frustrated by unfamiliar words and acronyms. Don't quit too soon. Give yourself a good six months to become familiar with the specialized language in your new area of interest. Soon your mind will begin to connect the dots and things will fall into place. When that happens, your interest in learning more about the subject will grow. Don't give up! The more we know about a topic, the more interesting it becomes.

3. Accept that your interests will change over time. I used to read everything I could find about managed health care. Only rarely do I look for items on that topic nowadays. You'll know when your tastes and needs have changed. Give yourself permission to move on.

4. Don't sweat it if you fall into a reading slump once in a while. I tend to read in streaks, devouring everything I can get my hands on for days and then not picking up anything for a week. Even for people who love it, reading can be a chore at times. When it feels that way, put it aside for a while but only for a little while.

"Reading is to the mind what exercise is to the body."
—Joseph Addison

Build a Powerful Vocabulary

There is a well-established correlation between a strong vocabulary and success. Interestingly enough, according to Margaret E. Broadley, an authority on human aptitude, "Only about

3,500 words separate the high vocabulary person from the low. Yet these 3,500 words can make the difference between success and failure."

When you come across a word you don't know, write it down and look it up as soon as you can. It doesn't take long to do it, yet you will rapidly increase your vocabulary by making a special effort to notice these words and learn them.

Every so often pick up an audiotape or book like *Verbal Advantage* by Charles Harrington Elster. Similar aids can be found on the Web. In fact, you might want to check out vocabulary-building Web sites like *www.Vocabulary.com* as well.

Tedious? Perhaps, but the benefits are fabulous. Your ability to understand what others are really saying will greatly improve. When you need to make a critical point, having the exact word at your command is powerful. A word of caution: Words can also be weapons. Don't use words solely to impress or to intimidate your listeners. Such behavior is abusive and it certainly won't increase your sales.

Finally, take the time to learn the correct pronunciation of the words you learn. President George W. Bush is occassionally lampooned for his mispronunciation of words. The President of the United States can probably turn that foible into an advantage, because it appears as though he is a regular guy, but you don't have that luxury. If you mangle the pronunciation of certain words, you are probably better off not using them. People notice mispronunciations, although they will rarely correct you.

"Why do large vocabularies characterize executives and possibly outstanding men and women in other fields? The final answer seems to be that words are the instruments by means of which men and women grasp the thoughts of others and with which they do much of their own thinking. They are the tools of thought."
—Johnson O'Connor

Join Toastmasters

If you really want to improve your presentation skills, I suggest you join Toastmasters International. With nearly 9,000 Toastmasters clubs worldwide, chances are there is a club in your community. Toastmasters is an organization, dedicated to improving communication and leadership skills. Toastmasters Clubs give you an opportunity to experiment with your style, test your latest presentation, and overcome weaknesses in a risk-free supportive environment. You'll have ample opportunity to deliver prepared talks as well as gain exposure to extemporaneous and impromptu speaking situations. Members offer each other constructive evaluation at each meeting, and it's a great confidence builder.

Successful people from all walks of life have improved their communication skills through Toastmasters. Well-known business leaders like Harvey Mackay, bestselling author of *Swim with the Sharks Without Being Eaten Alive,* sports figures like tennis champion Billie Jean King, and government leaders like Senator Sam Nunn have all benefited from Toastmasters membership.

As a longtime member of Toastmasters, I have noticed that each club has a unique personality. Many communities have more than one club to choose from. Visit several before choosing to join. Then, make a 100 percent commitment for at least one year. You will never regret it. To find a club near you and learn more about Toastmasters, check out their Web site at *www.Toastmasters.org.*

> *"The ability to express a thought is well nigh as important as the thought itself."*
> —Bernard Baruch

Watch Other People Communicate

I know. It sounds perfectly obvious. Yet, if you don't deliberately make a point of observing the way other people communicate, you will likely miss some superb insights. A man I worked for at Blue Cross was perhaps the most skilled communicator I have ever met. He taught me the importance of rehearsal before a presentation.

He showed me how to share a speaker's platform with a celebrity without being upstaged. He even showed me how to handle a barrage of insults without losing my composure or lowering myself to my competitor's level.

We were meeting with a well-known physician to discuss his proposal for a pain management program. The doctor had a reputation for bullying people. My boss was trying to explain why we couldn't approve his program without some important changes. The doctor was not used to being told no. He had two staff members with him and he decided to put on a show, accusing my boss of lying and implying that he wasn't very bright. My boss never raised his voice. He tried to reason with the doctor but nothing worked. The doctor got louder as he added more insults.

Finally my boss said, "Well, I've been insulted, and I've been called a liar. No one has ever done that to me before. I think it's time for me to leave." Understand that the meeting was taking place in our conference room. He then turned to the other attendees and said, "Thank you for coming. I'm sorry we couldn't get more done today." With that he left. So did the doctor.

My boss could have gotten into a shouting match. Certainly he could have hurled a few insults in the doctor's direction. But he understood that under the circumstances, quiet reasoning was the right approach. He kept trying until it was obvious to everyone in the room that the doctor was the problem. He could have asked the doctor to leave, but his approach, while subtle, had the desired effect. I can still see the doctor, tail between his legs, rapidly walking to the elevator.

Three months later the doctor got his program. He made the changes we requested. He also behaved himself.

It pays to actively observe the way your coworkers, customers, and superiors communicate. Likewise as a consumer, you can observe the way people sell to you. Make a conscious effort to observe the way a retail salesperson handles your inquiries. You encounter sales situations every day. Make the most of these moments. From the salesperson at Sears to your real estate agent, people are making sales talk. Are they communicating effectively? Is there a better way to say it? What reaction did they get? Was the reaction desirable under the circumstances?

▶*Watch other people. Listen and learn.*

Self-Talk

Self-talk is an often-ignored form of communication. Yet, self-talk is probably more responsible for our success or lack of it than any other form of communication. What you say to yourself shapes your self-image. If you tell yourself *I'm no good at cold calls* enough times, you will eventually have trouble picking up the phone. Sending the brain negative messages over and over again guarantees negative results.

On the other hand, positive messages work the same way. By reinforcing positive thoughts and images, you can greatly improve your performance and sales results. Would you rather walk into a sales presentation thinking, "These people are probably not very interested in our services. The last guy sure wasn't interested. Maybe I can get in and out in thirty minutes." Or, would you rather say, "I have something that can really help these people get what they need, and I'm going to prove it." Which thought is more likely to produce a sale?

Self-talk is an accurate predictor of performance. Whether silent thoughts or spoken words, what you believe about yourself is ultimately what you will be. If you tend to be critical of yourself, you need to stop what you're doing and reprogram your thoughts. There are numerous books and tapes on the subject of self-talk. If negative self-talk is an issue for you, by all means invest in one of these books.

"Inside myself is a place where I live all alone and that's where you renew your springs that never dry up."
—Pearl S. Buck

Chapter 2

Getting Ready to Tell Your Story

How Well Do You Know Your Product?

As a customer who is called on nearly every day by salespeople, I am no longer surprised when a salesperson doesn't seem to know his or her own products or services. On the other hand, when I did sales training, I learned that although many sales professionals do know their products, they simply don't know how to explain them. Sales representatives often have difficulty articulating the features and benefits of their products.

Occasionally, the fault lies with the product itself. I can distinctly remember training a group that was trying to sell among other things, a "sophisticated" data report. Each member of the group tried to describe its features and benefits, and each told a substantially different story. After probing for a while, I discovered the problem. No one was able to grasp the uniqueness of the report. They were stumbling because they were unsure of the report's purpose. Once we clarified its value to the customer, they all were able to enthusiastically describe the report.

In today's competitive market, shooting from the hip and glad-handing don't work anymore. The key to effective sales is preparation. The following list of suggestions will help you be the best you can be.

- *Know your product so well you can describe it in your sleep.* Start by reading the company's marketing literature. If there are product specifications, read those too. Don't expect training, delivered by your manager or other staff members, to be enough. Too often it isn't. If possible, use the product or service yourself. Observe it being used by others. You may even be surprised to discover features and benefits that are not mentioned in the literature.

- *Talk to customers.* Ask them what they like about your product or service. What concerns do they have? Not only will they teach you something you didn't know about the product, they can provide you with insights and stories that become terrific product endorsements you can use in your sales presentation to the next customer.

- *Believe in the product.* It sounds obvious, doesn't it? Why sell something you don't believe in? Yet, when you start a new job selling a product or service you aren't really familiar with, you are forced to make some assumptions, giving the company and its product the benefit of the doubt. In fact, most of us begin with unbridled enthusiasm. Never assume, however, that your new company or its products are completely worthy of that enthusiasm. Real confidence in products and services and the company producing them is earned over time.

- *Check out the product for yourself.* It's easy to say, "We make the best quality computer monitors in the industry," or "Our service department is the friendliest in town." After all, it's in your marketing literature. As a sales professional though, you have an obligation to be sure. It takes time, but if you begin to have doubts, it will show up in your presentation. Trust your instincts. At some point you will know the truth.

▶*You must believe in what you sell. Only then will you really own your presentation.*

14

How Is Your Product Positioned?

Product positioning is a marketing term that describes how your product is positioned in the marketplace. For our purposes, as you develop your sales presentation, I want you to consider how your product is positioned in your customer's mind. Start by checking your company's marketing literature and press releases to tell you something about how the company sees itself and its products. You also need to know how your customers view your product. To find out, ask them.

Knowing how your product is positioned in the customer's mind allows you to tailor your presentation, reinforcing strong areas and addressing any perceived weak spots. Does your company have a reputation for excellent service? Are you known for good quality but high prices? Knowing where you stand will help you craft an effective presentation. Not knowing decreases your chances of making a sale.

Positioning often becomes an issue when a company introduces a new product line. A company that is well known and respected for a particular product or service decides to take advantage of its brand to roll out an entirely new and different line. Several years ago, the makers of Jack Daniels whiskey introduced Jack Daniels beer. It had the terrific Jack Daniels brand going for it. It was a quality product. Yet, it didn't sell. Why? No one associates Jack Daniels with beer. Although this is perhaps an extreme case, at some point in your career you will probably be asked to sell a new product designed to help your company break into a new market.

It's a tough assignment. However, your chances of success will be much improved if you understand where your customers have placed your company in their minds to begin with. You can build your presentation with a clearer understanding of what you really need to accomplish.

Understanding how your company and its products are

positioned in the customer's mind can save you a lot of time and heartache. If you want to learn more about positioning, I highly recommend any of the books written on the subject by Al Ries and Jack Trout.

> ▶*Know how your product is positioned,*
> *then make it work for you.*

Develop an Organized Presentation

Recently, a national accounts manager representing a major international corporation called on me, hoping to persuade me to switch to his company's products. We had a long-standing relationship with our current supplier. We were very familiar with our current supplier's equipment and we had a lot of their product in inventory. Even more problematic, we had hundreds of customers using their products. A conversion to an alternative source would have been daunting for us. Certainly we would need a very good reason to switch.

What did the national accounts manager do? In spite of the fact that he was well aware of these issues, the accounts manager spent the first thirty minutes describing *how* they would help us make the conversion. He minimized the obstacles we would encounter, making it sound as though we would hardly notice the change.

Finally, somewhat frustrated, I asked him if he could explain *why* we should switch. As I said, we would need a compelling reason. His response, while not entirely convincing, wasn't necessarily a deal killer. Regardless, the path he chose, explaining the logistics before he made the sale, made me worry about those issues rather than see the benefits that might make the task worthwhile.

Good organization skills and the ability to see things in logical order are essential to successful selling. A well-organized presentation gives you a reliable road map, guaranteeing that you tell your story every time.

In the real world of selling, you rarely have the opportunity to tell your whole story in an uninterrupted monologue. In fact, it shouldn't be your goal to do so. You want to have a conversation with your customers. Like any conversation, there are questions, diversions, and tangents that pop up and must be addressed. However, unless you have a firm grasp of your overall purpose and direction, precious time with your customer can evaporate. Suddenly you are saying goodbye, with your objectives still trapped in your briefcase.

Every well-organized presentation has three parts: an opening, a body, and a close. Each part has a specific job.

The Opening

Your opening is designed to get your customer's attention and let the staff know your reason for meeting with them. Your opening also gives your audience a chance to get to know you. When I was selling home care services, I usually started with a story about a patient. Why? Human interest, of course, but it was also a way to pull my clients (usually HMOs) out of their customary world in which decisions were often made based on cold, hard, and impersonal data.

I got their attention by telling a good story. I told them how the patients we served were affected by their disease states. I explained how our service helped patients recover in the comfort of their homes and how the HMO could play a critical role in the process by paying for our services. I showed them how what they did, however remote from the patient's life, mattered a great deal. All of this was true. It would have been useless, if not devastating, to fabricate a tearjerker in an effort to manipulate my clients.

My story performed four tasks. First, it got their attention. Second, I used it to tell the customer something important about what my company did. Third, I wove my purpose for the meeting into the story, which gave me a terrific jumping-off point to the body of my presentation. Finally, I put my customers into the story, giving them an important role.

The Body

The body of a sales presentation should make your case. Explain the features and benefits of your products and services. Again, when I sold home care services, I offered three primary features. I emphasized personal service, the lower cost of home care when compared to hospitalization, and clinical expertise. I related the benefits to both patients and payer sources. I also used pertinent statistics, studies, and more stories to support my message.

I also used the body of my presentation to address any concerns I had uncovered previously.

The Close

I always closed my presentations by re-emphasizing my key points. I often found it effective to loop back to my opening story to revisit the key points that demonstrate how my services made a difference, briefly re-emphasizing key features and benefits. Finally, I asked the customer for the business.

Organizing your sales presentation gives you a solid framework for delivering a solid presentation. Take the time to write a complete script of your presentation. You should do at least three drafts to be sure you have all the facts and selling points organized so your story can be understood. If you want to be sure your presentation is thorough, practice it in front of a colleague. Then try it in front of someone outside your industry. Their feedback will help you uncover any problems.

Writing a well-organized presentation ensures that you will include the essential points that all customers need to hear. But that's only the beginning. Every customer is unique. To some extent, you must customize your approach to fit each customer's preferences and needs.

By doing your homework before you meet with your client and by asking good questions during your meeting, you will soon be adept at adjusting your pitch to accommodate the situation. We'll discuss these points in more detail in the next section.

Your sales presentation requires regular updating to keep it fresh. As you become more comfortable with it, keep in mind that being entertaining can be a big plus. Learn to build in a few laugh lines, poking good-natured fun at yourself or even your product if it's appropriate.

▶*Organize your presentation so you deliver the message your customer needs to hear.*

Brevity (Less Can Be More)

Brevity in sales presentations is critical. Tomorrow morning, watch the commercials on CNN. You'll notice that most of them run either fifteen or thirty seconds. A lot of information is packed into those seconds. Our society has gotten used to getting information in small bites. Look at *USA Today.* You'll notice it's filled with short articles containing just the facts. Attention spans are short and getting shorter. If you can't tell your story quickly and succinctly, you are in trouble.

How long should your presentation be? Since your presentation can't provide the slick and expensive (photography, choreographed music, attractive models, voice-over, etc.) production effects that TV commercials have, you need more time to get your point across. Work on it until you have a thirty-minute presentation with fifteen- and twenty-minute versions to fit the circumstances. Remember, if customers want more, they'll ask for it.

"Let thy speech be short, comprehending much in few words."
—Apocrypha, Ecclesiasticus 32:8

Tape Your Presentation

Zig Ziglar, the famous motivational speaker, says you aren't really in the world of selling unless you tape your presentation and play it back. Why is it so important to hear yourself selling? First, taping yourself is a great way to practice. Each time you listen to yourself deliver your presentation, you will notice changes you want to make *and* you will see improvements.

As you practice your presentations, you'll discover that your voice will project more confidence. It may feel strange at first, sitting all alone in a room, pretending to address a customer while you're actually looking at a bookcase or a refrigerator. You may not like the sound of your voice on tape. Don't obsess over it. Concentrate on the task at hand.

Listen for the following:

- Are there certain words you tend to use frequently? So frequently they could become a distraction to your listeners? Listen for filler words and phrases like "it has a programmable monitor *and everything.*" Words like *stuff, you know, like,* as in, "This is *like* unique to the industry." If you want to sound confident and knowledgeable, eliminate filler words from your vocabulary.
- Are you dropping the endings of certain words? Does your voice trail off just when you should be raising it for emphasis?
- Are you leaving out some important points? Is your message easy to follow or are you talking randomly, jumping from a key feature, to price, to an upgraded version of the product?
- As you begin to get more comfortable, experiment with different approaches. Listen to yourself. If your voice sounds

monotone, try raising it and lowering it. Have some fun and exaggerate your intonation. You may be surprised to learn that your idea of exaggeration is not, in reality, far from what it should actually be. Try speeding up and slowing down your rate of speech. Place emphasis on different words and phrases. Soon, you will discover ways to add impact to your message. A word of caution: Don't rehearse so much that your words sound memorized or mechanical. Your goal is to evaluate and improve your performance not to develop a one-act play.

▶*Tape yourself and discover how much you can improve.*

Pre-Call Communication Planning

Sales experts will tell you quite correctly that you need to plan out your sales calls in detail. Doing so greatly improves your chances of success. Let's say you have three objectives on your next call. You want to respond to a problem raised at your last meeting, introduce a new product, and discuss your client's tendency to stretch payment terms.

Certainly it's important to know your objectives, but a critical part of your pre-call planning must include your communication strategy.

Looking at the agenda, the first question that would occur to me is how much time does the customer have? Also, based on my knowledge of the customer, what is their attention span? The third, and most critical, question is how are you ranking the importance of each item?

If your concern about slow payment, for example, is really a priority, you may want to reconsider introducing your new product that day. Why? In the customer's mind, your sales message is going to get mixed in with your collection efforts. You can separate the events in your mind but don't count on the customer's ability to compartmentalize so easily. You never want to link a negative thought to your product.

Now let's assume that once you've thought about it, your real reason for the visit is to introduce a new product or program. Once that's clear, it becomes much easier for you to plan a communication strategy. Getting the problems solved and off your customer's plate is the best way to get their full attention. Then you can launch into your new product.

Thinking creatively about your communication strategy in advance will improve your chances of making a good impression on your customer. Sometimes you can even turn a negative situation into a plus. Remember that while you make a lot of sales calls every day, you must prepare for each one individually. Don't fall into the trap of treating each new sales call as an extension of the last one. Each encounter is a new and unique interaction. Your communication strategy will be different on each call.

▶ *You'll make more sales if you make your communication strategy a part of your pre-call planning routine.*

Scheduling an Appointment

Scheduling an appointment is something most salespeople take for granted. The conversation goes something like this:

"Hi Len, it's Marie from Maxiflo. I was wondering if I could stop by next Thursday and tell you a little bit about our new oxygen device. Would ten o'clock work for you?"

If I have an established relationship with the supplier, there's a good chance I'll give the caller an appointment. Still, I'm just as likely to try to put the meeting off or to get someone on my staff to handle the meeting. Why? For one thing, the salesperson hasn't put as much thought as they could into the call.

Marie is under the mistaken impression that if she makes it sound as though this meeting won't take much of my time, I will bc more likely to schedule it. Actually the opposite is true. I want to spend my time on things that can make a meaningful difference to our company. If it's no big deal, why bother?

With just a little homework on her part and by consciously thinking about her communication strategy, Marie could make the prospect of a meeting much more interesting for me. If she said, "Len, it's Marie from Maxiflo. I have some information for you. In just the past six months, you've bought fifteen hundred of our EvenFlo oxygen devices. We just introduced a redesigned product, the EvenFlo Plus, which can save you quite a bit of money. I took the liberty of showing it to your Dallas branch. They're buying most of the EvenFlo's now. They liked it and suggested I discuss it with you. Are you available at ten o'clock next Thursday?"

In this scenario, the salesperson gave me some important information to help me decide to see her. I now know specifically how much of this product we are buying. She is offering to save me money in the future. Since the actual users of the product appear to have endorsed it, more time may be saved in testing and evaluation. I'll meet with Marie, if for no other reason than I know she won't waste my time.

Many sales situations involve much more complex transactions. Even when the salesperson has made a convincing argument about why we should meet, too often, vendors come to the meeting unprepared. Their reason for being there isn't clear.

I remember a meeting with the senior management of a New York–based technology firm. It took a great deal of effort for both of us to get the meeting date, time, and location nailed down. One week before the meeting, he called me to ask what I wanted to cover. I outlined three things I wanted to see.

First, I asked for a demonstration of their product. Second, since they were bringing along a consultant from an internationally renowned firm, I asked them to prepare for an exchange of ideas and concepts that might help us in our quest to identify the best Web-based procurement program to suit our needs. Third, since they were a start-up organization, I requested an update on their financial status. At this point, he should have indicated how much time he would need to adequately cover these topics. He never addressed it. When I put the meeting on my calendar, I assumed we would need about two hours.

The vendor started the meeting by letting me know that while he expected we would be meeting all day, the "fact" that I would only be available for two hours required him to change the agenda. He would have to skip the demo as a result. I asked him how he got the impression we would be meeting all day. He wasn't sure. Then he had a hard time explaining the actual role the consultant's firm would play in our relationship. The financial information he offered was fuzzy at best. It was not a productive meeting.

Still, I couldn't help thinking that we could have achieved something if we all had had a clear understanding in advance of the time required to achieve our objectives. I was partly to blame for the failure, of course. But I was the customer. I didn't spend $2,000 to fly two people to the meeting. It only cost me about two hours.

If you are not organized and on top of your meeting planning, how much confidence should a customer place in your assertion that your firm can deliver a quality product or service? You are always communicating something to the customer. Are you sending the message you intended to send?

As a sales professional, you are obligated to clearly communicate your intentions to the customer. You should address these issues:

* *How much time does the customer have for the meeting?* When you meet with the customer, confirm your understanding of the amount of time available. Situations can

change schedules unexpectedly. It's better to know that early in the meeting so you can make adjustments if necessary.

- *Ask who will be attending the meeting: Get their names, titles, and the reason they will be there.* This kind of intelligence can help you determine the agenda and might give you some insight about how seriously the customer is considering your service. Let the customer know who will be joining you from your organization.
- *If a representative from another firm who is working in partnership with you will also be attending, be sure to explain to your customer why the representative is coming.* Let your customer know the nature of the relationship between your organization and the other firm. Make certain that your customer has no objections to having a third party join in.
- *Review the agenda with the customer, including the topics and their purpose.* Get agreement on each topic.
- *If you will be using audiovisual aids, let the customer know.* Make sure they have a room that will accommodate your presentation. Perhaps they have some of the equipment you will need so you don't have to bring everything with you.

When you are sure you have agreement on the topic and the logistics of the meeting, put it in writing. One of the many benefits of e-mail is that you can quickly send off a note highlighting your conversation and get a quick confirmation back from the customer.

▶*It pays to be thorough when you schedule an appointment.*

Your Place or Mine?

In most situations, you meet with customers at their location. However, there are times when you might want to invite the customer in to see your operation. Site visits can be an excellent strategy, provided you have taken into account the communication factor.

When I was working for Blue Cross in provider contracting, health care providers called on me regularly, seeking a contract so they could provide services to our members. In most instances I insisted on meeting in my office because it saved me precious time. Meeting at their location could easily cost me three hours including the round trip to and from the office. In hindsight, I should have traveled to the customer's location more often.

There isn't any substitute for seeing the place you are doing business with. You can learn something about their culture, financial status, and operational efficiency just by taking a tour of their facilities.

Before you invite customers to your office or plant, keep in mind that they may have a mental picture of what your facilities look like even if they've never seen it. Experience and imagination, as well as their impression of you personally, contribute to their mind's eye view of your firm. Before you invite them to see your place there are several important factors you should take into consideration:

- Has the customer ever been to your office or plant before?
- What condition is your facility in? Does it need paint? Is it so lavish that they might wonder whether your prices are too high?
- Have they seen your competitor's place?
- How does your facility compare with your competitor's? If your competitor has better facilities, it's better to let your customer assume yours looks the same.
- Is the customer likely to leave your location feeling more or less confident about your company's capabilities?

- Be sure that everyone in the office knows you have guests coming. If you don't have facilities you can brag about, you can have the most well groomed staff in sight.
- Be a gracious host. Make sure there are plenty of refreshments but don't go overboard with high-cost goodies.
- Even an office or plant needing a paint job can be cleaned up of papers, boxes, computer monitors, and keyboards piled against the wall and pictures on cubicle walls that suggest a nervous breakdown would be an improvement over working here.
- If your facilities are a bit tired looking, unless you're in the middle of renovations, don't apologize for your surroundings. There's no need to call attention to the obvious. Instead, focus on the value of your product and your company's enthusiasm in serving its customers.

Sometimes you don't have a choice. The customer insists on meeting at your location. Whether your facility is the Ritz or a warehouse badly in need of renovation, good preparation can make an enormous difference to the outcome of the meeting.

▶*Sometimes a picture really is worth a thousand words.*

Chapter 3

Your Presentation Tools

Passion

After the events of September 11, the American people had a substantially different opinion of President George W. Bush's leadership. Prior to the catastrophe various pundits questioned whether he was up to the job. During the days and weeks immediately following the crisis though, he demonstrated leadership in many ways, including a newfound eloquence. When he delivered his State of the Union message the following January, reviewers gave him high marks for his words on terrorism. They were less complimentary about the portion of his speech that focused on the economy. When it came to foreign policy, he was called eloquent and powerful in his words. On domestic policy, some said he was less than forthright and disappointing.

Anyone who saw the President's speech could see the difference in his tone and demeanor when he switched from the war on terrorism to domestic policy. The President had a clear mission to root out terrorism. It was obvious in his words and actions that he meant business.

When you meet with your customers, are you on a mission? Are you completely confident that what you are selling offers a significant improvement over what the customer is doing now? The answer has to be yes if you are going to successfully use your communication skills. Eloquence is a wonderful attribute, but conviction is what sells your client. It can't be faked. Without it, all the eloquent words become practically worthless.

If you don't fully believe in your product or service, it will show. If you are not in love with what you sell now, there are three things you can do to achieve a maximum level of commitment. First, learn everything you can about your products and services. Understand their weaknesses as well as their strengths and what your company is doing to improve them. Knowledge is indeed power. Second, find out what customers really think. If they love what you sell, find out what they love about it so you can confidently relate the facts to your prospects. Third, if possible, use the product yourself. Firsthand knowledge will dramatically increase your enthusiasm. If you are still feeling lukewarm after you've taken these steps, think about making a change. Find something that really turns you on. Being passionate gives you credibility. It breeds enthusiasm. It sells.

> *"Nothing great in the world has been accomplished without passion."*
>
> —Hegel

Watch That Tone of Voice

When you were a child and your mother said, "Watch that tone of voice," you knew you were about to cross the line. The tone of *her* voice sent that message loud and clear. We use our voices to convey a wide range of emotions. Fear, love, concern, and anger, as well as positive and negative attitudes, can easily be detected in our tone of voice.

Voice tone is determined by pitch, which refers to your vocal range—the highs and lows of your voice. Most people have a range of less than two octaves. However, there is plenty of room to make effective use of your voice within that range. Imagine being at a surprise party where everyone says, "surprise!" just as the guest of honor enters the room. The emphasis and impact are usually on the last part of the word, or *prise;* the voices go into the higher ranges as they complete the word.

Now imagine the same situation, only this time, picture everyone saying the word with no emphasis as if they were repeating the word after having spelled it in a spelling bee. Not very exciting, is it?

You can learn to use your voice to help you make key points during your sales presentations and your informal conversations with customers. Remember, raising your voice when you want to drive home a key point is not always the most effective way to communicate with customers. Lowering your voice is often more effective.

To make effective use of your voice, it has to be natural. Observe people whose communication skills you admire. Usually, they are relaxed and confident. And remember—no amount of practice will help you use your voice effectively if you don't believe what you are saying.

▶*Your voice is an instrument. Learn to play it well.*

Speech Rate

Sales professionals who sell to physicians are familiar with this drill. You stand in the corridor waiting for the doctor to finish another conversation. As he breaks free, you run up and find yourself walking down the hall with him, trying to hold his attention. You think, "I have to make this fast before I lose him." So you rush your words, trying to cram in as much information as possible about your company and your products. There's a good chance that in the rush to say it all, you leave out certain bits of key information.

How fast should you talk? Most of us speak between 120 and 160 words per minute. Under the pressure of a sales presentation, you may be talking faster than your normal rate of speech.

Your speech rate can have a significant impact on how you are perceived and how much of what you say is really being absorbed. Speaking too fast might actually raise doubts about you, unless you have already built credibility with the customer. We all know the cliché about the fast-talking car salesman. We suspect he's trying to blow something by us before we realize what's happened. Regardless of what you're selling, talking fast doesn't usually work in your favor. Even if your customers are eager to hear what you are saying, they might not be able to keep up with you.

On the other hand, speaking too slowly might cause your customers to lose interest. While you mosey through your presentation, they may be drifting off, worrying about their golf game or their to-do list.

Use these three easy suggestions to improve your speech:

1. *Speak at a rate of speed that matches the point you are making.* Consider the difference between listening to a baseball game and a hockey game. The announcers speak at different rates to describe what is happening. So should you.

2. *Vary your speech rate to emphasize key points.* You can move more quickly through items that are generally well known to your audience. Slow down as you describe key features and benefits with which your customer is less familiar.

3. *When you are pressed for time, focus on one or two key points.* What is your most important point? Say it, reinforce it, and get out of the way. Your customer will appreciate it. He'll remember it too.

▶*Think fast. Speak to be understood.*

The Refreshing Pause

The pause is an art form well worth cultivating. Used appropriately, it adds impact to your presentation, signals confidence, and increases the likelihood that you will be understood. When you think about it, a pause is really a moment of silence. Most people have a fear of silence, both in business situations and in everyday conversations. Yet, once this fear is conquered, you can add the pause to your arsenal of effective communication tools. To overcome any concerns you may have about a moment of silence, recognize that a pause isn't nearly as long as it seems. Usually, a pause only lasts between one and three seconds. But even a longer pause lasting seven or eight seconds is acceptable.

A pause is a marvelous alternative to fillers like *ahh, uhm,* or *you know.* We tend to make these sounds or say these words because they eliminate the momentary silence. Instead of using these words, try to pause deliberately and with purpose. You will not feel uncomfortable, and your words will have more impact.

Pauses are effective in these situations:

- *Pause to introduce a new idea.* A pause provides a natural breaking point for a transition
- *Pause after you have made a particularly important point.* A pause gives your listeners a chance to absorb what you just said. For example, in his famous quote about the Great Depression, President Franklin D. Roosevelt said, "The only thing we have to fear is *(pause)* fear itself."
- *Pause after you show someone a visual.* Have you ever been frustrated when someone hands you a report or brochure to review, or perhaps shows you a slide, and continues to talk so you can't really focus on what's in your hand? Give your customer time to absorb visuals before you speak.
- *Pause before answering a question.* Give yourself time to collect your thoughts. Pausing to think before you respond

signals that you think enough of the question to give a thoughtful answer.

- *Pause if your listeners appear distracted or if they're not really paying attention.* Sometimes a deliberate pause will bring them back. In essence you are asking them to pay attention.
- *Extend the pause as an effective way to close a sale.* Once you have asked for a commitment from the buyer, remain silent until you get an answer. Consider it an extended pause if you like. Resist the urge to begin talking to break the silence. Give the customer time to think. By all means, answer any questions but keep your replies brief. If necessary, reiterate your request for an order. Then calmly wait for a response.

> *"I believe in the discipline of silence and could talk for hours about it."*
> —George Bernard Shaw

How to Use Your Marketing Literature

To some sales professionals, marketing literature is an afterthought. At times, it's even referred to as a "leave behind." Yet your marketing literature is unique as a communication tool because it is written, edited, tested, and sharpened to ensure that you send your message exactly the way you want it sent. Good marketing literature can help you achieve your sales goals in several ways.

Build Credibility

When you give your customer a glossy brochure, it sends a message that you represent a going concern. It is one of those things that people mentally check off about a company they are thinking of doing business with. Obviously, this isn't important if you are dealing with a well-known company with an established reputation. It does matter when they've never heard of you.

Educate Yourself

Marketing literature is also useful as an educational aid to the sales professional. After reviewing your firm's marketing material, you should be able to understand what your company does as well as the features and benefits of its products.

Sometimes your company's marketing literature isn't very clear. That should alert you that you have some homework to do. Don't assume that there isn't a better way to promote your products than what your marketing brochure says.

I can remember trying to learn all about home care services in my first sales job. The support material was long on flowery stories about getting patients healthy, which I hasten to add, was not a bad thing. But I needed something that would show managed-care organizations the intricacies of actually delivering patient care at home. It was important because our services weren't cheap. I needed ammunition to support the high cost of our services. The company I worked for had nothing that would help me perform that task.

I spoke with the pharmacists, nurses, and warehouse and billing staff to help me understand the behind-the-scenes efforts necessary to ensure good patient care. They explained the complexity of serving patients at home. Then I developed my own support materials to help me overcome a serious objection to the sale.

A Selling Tool

If your brochure is suitable for the purpose, walk the customer through it. It's surprising how infrequently sales representatives do this. In fact, a review of the brochure may be the only time a customer really looks at it. I am not suggesting a line-by-line, word-for-word review. Hit the highlights. It's a great way to make sure you don't miss something important, especially if you are just starting out in sales. Pay attention to the customer's signals. If they start fidgeting or showing other signs of distraction, wrap it up and move on to other items on your agenda.

▶*Put your marketing literature to work for you.*

Visual Aids

Visual aids are terrific sales tools if you remember that every interaction with a customer is an important communication event. Your choice of visual aids helps customers shape their opinion of you and your company. From graphic design to color selection, your choices say something about you and your company.

The visual aids you use say something about your opinion of the customer, too. For example, have you ever seen overheads with spelling errors in them? Have you ever witnessed a presentation filled with colors and pictures that Generation X'ers would love in a room filled with baby boomers?

When you use visuals, make sure you are thinking as carefully about your media selection as you would the content of your presentation. A crisp and entertaining presentation communicates to your customer that you value them. It shows them you went to a great deal of thought and trouble to make it special for them.

Let's take a moment to define the term *visual aids*. Traditionally, visual aids are low-tech items, meaning anything from flip charts to overheads. Although any of these aids can serve your purposes well, today we also have options like PowerPoint presentations that can be viewed via an LCD projector from your laptop. We can now enhance our presentations with a dazzling array of sounds, motion, and crisp graphics not available in the past. Today, when we say visual aids, we are really talking about multimedia presentations.

Regardless of the technology available, consider whether

your presentation really needs visual aids. Visual aids tend to work better in some situations than in others. Generally, they are more effective in these situations:

In front of larger audiences—Knowing the size of your audience can help you determine which medium to use. Smaller audiences, up to five or six people, tend to be less formal. Here, handouts, flip charts, and overheads are fine.

A larger audience usually expects something more formal than a smaller audience. Visual aids tend to make presentations more formal. The more technology you use, the more formal the presentation becomes.

If you are selling to a large audience, controlling the flow of the meeting can be more difficult. One advantage of using multimedia is that it helps you maintain the control necessary to get your message out. People are more likely to sit and listen politely if you are standing in front of them with a prepared talk.

In larger rooms—It is important to know the size of the room you will be working in. Call ahead and ask your customer about the meeting room. Find out what the room's dimensions are. If, for example, you will be in a very small room, you may be better off with handouts or a flip chart rather than slides. A larger room—one that has enough space and room for a screen—is ideal for slides or Web site demonstrations. Be sure that your visuals are large enough for your audience to see without difficulty. Visuals they can't read are infinitely worse than no visuals at all.

When you have a lot of material to cover—If you have a product or service that requires some detailed explanations, multimedia can simplify matters and help clarify key points or issues. Carefully crafted slides that mix graphics with text can help you tell your story. To keep your audience with you, give it to them in bite-size pieces on the big screen. In this situation, I would avoid handouts. They tend to result in sidebar conversations. Many people can't resist flipping ahead to the next page. Give them your literature after your presentation is finished. One exception to this rule: A handout is fine if it's a copy of your slides formatted so that listeners can take notes adjacent to each slide.

Other Considerations

Time available—If you are using slides or overheads, as a rule of thumb, allow yourself two to two and one-half minutes per slide. Remember too that if you need equipment setup and teardown time, try to make arrangements to arrive early so you can have this taken care of before the meeting's scheduled start time. If the customer has a very tight time schedule, consider rescheduling for another day or go with less intrusive aids. I have seen enough people get antsy while waiting to get the darn projector to work right. Certainly, I prefer not to create my own obstacles to the sale. Respecting people's time is an important form of communication. Don't let your slide show ruin your sale.

Technology—Increasingly, we are using more technology in our presentations. It's true that technology offers many advantages including color, sound, and movement. There are several Web sites—such as *www.crystalgraphics.com* and *www.Presenters online.com*—that offer a variety of presentation aids including free downloads of sound and graphics. Be careful though, not to let the technical wizardry of your presentation overshadow your product or service. In other words, if your customer is so enthralled with asking, "How did you do that?" rather than focusing on your product, you've overdone it.

Find out what AV equipment is available at the client's location. Make sure it's compatible with any equipment you plan to bring along. Ask if there are sufficient electrical outlets and extension cords, and an Internet hookup if needed.

It's easy to get so focused on making a good impression that you forget these details. Trust me, once you have flown 1,000 miles, only to be forced to apologize for not having the equipment you need, you will never make that mistake again.

Naturally, technology has a few side effects. We've already mentioned the need to ensure that your customer can accommodate your electronic needs. But even in the best of circumstances, technology can fail. Glitches can be particularly devastating when you've assembled a large crowd, so be sure you have a backup plan when this happens. If you planned on a live demonstration of your Web site, be sure you have an offline demo that mirrors the essence of your live site.

Consider having a humorous observation ready just in case. It doesn't have to be a belly laugh. To reduce the tension in the room, consider saying something like this: "You know, the IT group warned me this would happen if I didn't buy them lunch. I didn't think they were serious."

Rehearsal—Recognize that using visual aids often means delivering a more formal presentation. Never make the mistake of assuming that your visuals are just notes for your talk. Their primary purpose is to add impact to your presentation and reinforce your message. If you don't know in advance what you are going to say, you might find yourself simply reading aloud what is on the screen, losing your audience in the process. You must rehearse what you are going to say with each visual you display. Make certain that your message is reinforced by the words or graphics on the screen.

▶*Media should be used to support your message. They aren't a substitute for good preparation or product knowledge.*

What's Your Energy Level?

If you don't have a high energy level and enthusiasm for your work, your customers will notice it. Remember that your customers interact with sales representatives every day. A low energy level can be detected in tone of voice, posture, how quickly you respond to requests, and in countless other ways, not the least of which is how you act compared to the salesperson your customer met with thirty minutes ago.

Yes, even energy level is a form of communication. Consciously, or worse, subconsciously, your customer will wonder why you don't seem enthusiastic, not to mention excited about your product. If you appear to be bored or distracted, it will be nearly impossible to generate the level of excitement your customer must feel if they are going to buy from you.

Remember too that enthusiasm is contagious. If you genuinely feel it, so will your customers. They can sense your confidence and commitment. I'm not suggesting that you talk loud and fast, bouncing off the walls. Being hyper makes people wary and ultimately turns them off. Your energy should be focused on your customer and your message. There are no secrets to having a high energy level. Start with what any doctor would tell you. Get enough rest, eat right, and exercise regularly. Build on that by making sure you sell something that turns you on.

Of course, no one has an endless supply of energy. That's why it pays to conserve it for when it counts. Build in some quiet time between calls. You don't have to check voice mail every time you jump in the car. Take time for lunch. Entertainers know exactly when to turn their energy up full force. They don't do it three hours before a scheduled appearance. They wait until they need it.

Occasionally even the best salesperson has a losing streak. Nothing seems to go right. Maybe you're not making sales or maybe a reorganization left your status in doubt. Then what?

You can fight your way through a slump by deliberately turning up the amps. By acting enthusiastic, you begin to feel enthusiastic. If that doesn't work, lay low for a day or so but no longer. Give yourself a chance to sort things out but remain positive. Soon, you'll feel rejuvenated with a fresh supply of energy to get you moving again.

> ▶*A high energy level can make up for*
> *a multitude of shortcomings.*

Chapter 4

The Sales Call

Get There on Time

If you have a two o'clock appointment, what time should you get there? It's been said that if you arrive at the appointed time, you're already late. Fair enough. But how early should you be? I say, five minutes. Here's why. If you arrive too early and have your arrival announced, your prospect has to either drop what he's doing or let you cool your heels in the lobby. Not much of a choice, is it? When someone calls on me fifteen or even thirty minutes early, I usually try to accommodate them, but I'm not necessarily happy about it. Being respectful of your customer's time says something positive about you. Why plant even little seeds of doubt?

Likewise, if you are going to be late for an appointment, tell your client you will be late the minute you know it. Briefly explain the problem and ask if they will bear with you. If you do business locally, offer to reschedule if you expect to be delayed by an hour or more. If you traveled a significant distance, try to persuade the customer to see you even if it's several hours later than planned. In most instances, customers will be sympathetic to your plight. Of course, if the customer can't rearrange his schedule, be gracious. Make another appointment for the earliest open date.

"Better never than late."
—George Bernard Shaw

That First Moment

In his book *You Are the Message*, Roger Ailes pointed out that research shows we begin to make up our minds about people we meet within seven seconds of meeting them. That's not a lot of time to make a good first impression. Under the circumstances, you can't afford to be careless about the way you greet your customer. A lot happens in those seven seconds.

Communication begins immediately when you meet someone. Your appearance speaks volumes before you utter your first word. There's no excuse for not being well groomed. Make a point of being meticulous about your appearance.

Are you smiling? You should be delighted to be there. You worked hard to get the appointment. No matter how your day has gone so far, regardless of what just happened ten minutes ago, you need to clear your mind of all distractions and focus on the moment. A genuine smile brightens the room.

As is the custom in the United States, shake hands with the people you meet. Offer a firm handshake and make eye contact. Forget the bone crusher your father taught you. Contrary to the myth that a hearty handshake suggests you are a person of substance, all it does in our aging population is trigger arthritis pain. Your handshake should convey warmth.

When you introduce yourself, use your voice to project confidence, warmth, and sincerity. Put your personality into it and enjoy the moment.

▶*Good beginnings make good endings.*

The Business Card Ritual

Exchanging business cards is a routine exercise. So routine in fact that we rarely give it a second thought. Yet, the card exchange is an important communication between you and your new customer. Your business card contributes to the kind of impression you make. Obviously, your business card should be clean and without creases. The print should be large enough to read without squinting. Unless you're in a business like advertising where your card can reflect the product or service you sell, stick to the essentials: your name, your title, and how to reach you. Avoid flashy designs that call attention to you rather than to your products or services.

Make sure you always have a supply of cards with you. Showing up at an appointment without a business card is unprofessional.

When the person you are meeting offers you his or her card, take a moment to look at it. Most of us barely glance at the other person's card before we slip it into a pocket or portfolio. In some cultures, such behavior is highly inappropriate.

In some Asian countries, for example, the business card is treated with great respect. When the card is offered, the recipient accepts it with both hands. If you travel internationally for business, learn the rituals each culture observes when exchanging cards. Be sure you know what the local custom is before you arrive at the meeting.

Regardless of where you're doing business, it's important to read the other person's card. Something on the card might surprise you. We've all seen unusual designs, colors, or titles that beg for an explanation. The prospect just may be handing you a built-in icebreaker. Don't miss the opportunity to take advantage of it. Keep the card in front of you during the meeting. That way you won't forget your customer's name. If the customer doesn't offer you a card, don't hesitate to ask for one.

Possibly they've simply forgotten to give you one. While we typically exchange business cards without much conscious thought, the act itself helps to create an impression, however subtle it may be. Don't take it for granted.

The Warm-Up

The goal of warming up your audience, whether it's an audience of one or twenty-five, is to set a tone conducive to accomplishing your goals. You want an audience that's receptive to your message. You want to start the process of earning their trust and the credibility of your company.

When a salesperson calls on me, I expect to spend at least a few minutes warming up. If we have never met before, I like to get comfortable with the person I'm dealing with before we move on to the business at hand. If I know the person calling on me, I want some time to get reacquainted.

Most salespeople have a standard topic or two that they use to get things warmed up. It might be a comment on the weather or a story describing the obstacles they surmounted traveling to their destination. Others prefer to pay a compliment, usually a vague reference to how nice the office is, or an observation about the attractive painting in the conference room. All of these options work as conversation starters. Certainly, they don't require much thought.

On the other hand, if you want to make a really strong impression, you'll have to spend some time analyzing the situation. Keeping good notes when you call on someone should include what the small talk was about. Why? You can build on what you learn about your customers in those moments. Maybe one of your customers loves boating or golf; maybe another owns a 1966 Mustang, loves the opera, or is a political junkie. What turns each of your customers on? During the warm-up phase of a meeting, probe a bit about their interests. Look for clues in office surroundings. Talk to their coworkers when the opportunity presents itself. If you take the time to learn about your customers, you can always have an interesting tidbit to open your meetings. Your customers will appreciate it and, even more important, look forward to seeing you.

The benefits of being observant and creative are many. For one thing, you will immediately set yourself apart from most of your competitors. Your customer will be impressed with your powers of observation. You may be surprised to learn how often you discover mutual interests or common ground from which to build a relationship. Don't be afraid to venture into unfamiliar terrain either. For example, I know nothing about boats or boating. But I do know how to ask questions. If a customer has a picture of an enormous sailboat, I want to know all about it. Here again, no faking allowed. Even if you don't particularly like boats, you can always learn something new. Remember your goal is to know the person. Pay attention to what excites them and you will discover their passion. The next time you see them, with a little homework on your part, you'll be prepared to really warm things up quickly.

How long should your warm-up be? Anything more than ten minutes is probably too long. In most situations, it's best to let the customer signal when they are ready to talk business. However, once you reach the ten-minute mark, you should gently take control and get the business meeting started if possible. Saying something like "I know how busy you are, and I have an idea I want to share with you" is an acceptable gambit.

▶*A good warm-up requires a warm person.*

Tell Me Something about Your Company

When a client says, "Tell me something about your company," it isn't a license to tell a long-winded story about how your company got started. Good novelists write an enormous amount that is never used in their novels to help them develop characters and motivation for their story. This information is called backstory. If writers imposed their entire backstory on their readers, they wouldn't be published.

When someone asks for your company's story, keep that in mind. Be ready with an edited version of your company's story and tell it. Keep your story short. Work on it until you can tell the story in five sentences or less. Stick to the basics, and if possible, refer to a current newsworthy event that demonstrates your organization's vitality.

Here's an example:

> *Office Plus is a publicly traded company that specializes in office supplies. We carry everything from pencils to easel pads to office furniture. We're based in Concord, California, and we have 225 service centers in forty states. In business for just seven years, we're the fastest growing office products company in the nation. Last month, we were awarded an exclusive contract to provide supplies to all government agencies in the state of New Jersey.*

If your firm is a brand-new start-up, you will want to provide additional information such as the names of the founder and the investors, assuming they are well known and respected in your industry. Add a few more details about the company's mission as well. A good rule of thumb for deciding what to include is to ask yourself how this information will help to move your sale forward.

The more well known your company is, the less information you need to offer. Of course you'll want to keep your customer up-to-date on recent positive developments within your company. Good news reaffirms your customer's decision to do business with you in the first place.

▶*Keep your company's story short.*
If customers want more, they'll ask for it.

Delivery

As we discussed earlier, an organized presentation has three distinct parts: an opening, a body, and a close. It is very important that you have full command of each part of your presentation.

Experienced salespeople know that they don't always get to deliver their message in the preferred order. There are unavoidable interruptions and questions that have a way of changing the direction of the discussion. That's fine. Your goal is to engage your customer in a conversation. There is a risk though that you can get so caught up in the dialogue that you forget to point out key aspects of your product. That's why you must know your presentation cold. When you know where you are going, it's easier to steer the discussion back on track after interruptions and sidebar conversations.

As you gain sales experience, you will become increasingly adept at customizing your presentation to fit each customer's preference. Some will want you to cut to the chase while others will expect every last detail about your company and its services. Remember the better you know your presentation, the easier it is to be flexible.

Key Points to Remember

- *Know your material thoroughly.* This frees your mind to listen carefully for questions and notice body language and other nuances that might give you useful clues about the impact you are making.
- *People tend to remember the first and last points and forget the middle.* That's why your presentation should emphasize

the key points you need to make early in your presentation. Repeat them at the end.

* *You've done a good job delivering your presentation if your client clearly understands what you do and why you are there.* One sign that you've reached them is the questions they ask. If they ask questions that require you to expand on what you've said, that's usually a good sign. Pay close attention to questions, objections, and observations the customer makes. They are clues that can help you improve your presentation and keep it fresh.

* *Your goal is to have a conversation with your customer but don't be casual.* You're giving a performance, and every night is opening night.

▶*Know your presentation cold. Deliver it like it's the first time, every time.*

Features and Benefits

Most of us are taught to sell the features of our products. Features describe the physical attributes or capabilities of a product such as color, gauges, speed settings, power, and so on. Most salespeople are reasonably adept at describing features. If they've read the literature and know the product, they can offer a great deal of information about it. Often, they will describe a product's features with great enthusiasm. But features rarely cause the customer to buy.

Benefits focus on what makes each feature useful to the customer. If you can persuade your customers that your product will help them make money, save money, save time, or enhance their status in some way, your chances of making the sale are greatly increased. When it comes to discussing benefits though, too many sales representatives come up short. Some never even get to the benefits. In spite of the fact that selling benefits is critical to sales success, too often benefits are glossed over. What's the best way to sell benefits?

Take time to understand why the marketing and research and development departments included each feature to begin with. They had a reason for doing so. Knowing why a feature exists will help you identify its benefits. For example, some computers come with a nonglare monitor. Customers benefit from this feature because they can see the screen regardless of the ambient lighting in the room.

Some benefits are universal, meaning that all buyers would benefit from them. However, don't assume that every feature is a benefit in your clients' eyes. The buyer, not the R&D department, ultimately determines value. Remember that one buyer's benefit is another's unnecessary expenditure. Take the time to learn more about your clients' motives in expressing interest in your product. Rest assured that whatever attributes catch their eyes they are envisioning benefits. Don't be afraid to ask why they like what they see. Likewise, don't assume that all customers can immediately see the benefits your product offers. That's one reason it's so important to be able to communicate benefits clearly. Discussing benefits really puts you in a consultative role. You aren't just selling; you're providing valuable assistance and offering thought-provoking ideas and observations.

You can communicate a benefit by taking an assumptive stance, saying, for example, "The twin hard drives will allow you to store twice the data in half the time." This approach works in situations where there is little room for doubt. However, there is always a risk that your client will disagree with your premise or simply state that neither the feature nor its benefit is useful. Momentarily you and your customer are at odds, which is certainly not your intention. A softer approach can be more effective. "Can you see that the twin hard drives might save you some time?" If the customer disagrees, it doesn't sound like a contradiction. You can ask a follow-up question to understand the difference of opinion or move on. Another approach to describing a benefit is to say, "What this means to you . . . " after you describe each benefit.

Match each feature with its benefits. Seek agreement on the benefits before moving on to the next feature. Make a point of asking the customer if he can see other benefits you haven't mentioned. You may well be surprised to discover that the customer is ahead of you or moving in a direction you never considered.

▶*Describe the features; discuss the benefits.*

Asking Questions

The ability to ask questions is an essential sales communication skill. Yet, salespeople don't ask enough questions. Even fewer ask the right questions. The information in this section will help you learn to ask the right questions.

There are several types of questions. Closed-ended questions usually elicit yes or no answers. Open-ended questions encourage people to talk. Each type serves a different purpose. Some questions are designed simply to gather information about the client's business. Others are meant to uncover problems; still others should address the consequences of those problems. Finally, there are questions that are designed to help customers reach the right solution to their problems.

Information-Gathering Questions

A lot of time is spent on sales calls gathering information that could easily have been obtained prior to the call. This is especially true today with the proliferation of company-sponsored Web sites. Many of them are bursting with useful information.

Although getting information about the status of your customer's business is very important, when you ask questions that could easily have been answered with a little research, you are communicating that you are lazy, you are not creative, and you don't value your customer's time.

Sound harsh? A few years ago I was speaking at a conference in San Diego. At lunch, I happened to sit next to a woman who had a reputation in the industry of being difficult. I knew it was true because I was trying to persuade her to meet with me, but I was not having much luck. During lunch we chatted about the differences she had observed over the years in sales techniques.

As someone representing an HMO with a dominant market share, she was much in demand. Hoping I could learn something, I asked her what frustrated her the most about meeting with salespeople. Without the slightest hesitation, she said, "I hate it when people ask me stupid questions. When they start out by asking me what our current enrollment is, I make sure it's a short meeting. I don't have time to do their homework for them. Our enrollment is public information. They should know that before they get there."

She may be a tough customer, but she has a point. Don't ask questions you should already know the answer to unless you need to verify the information. Then say something like "The last time I checked your enrollment was two-hundred and fifty thousand. Is that still accurate?"

Know what's going on in your customer's world before you get to their office. Although research alone won't always garner all the information you need, doing your homework has two advantages. First, your customer will notice that you're prepared, setting you apart from others. Second, the questions you ask will be more insightful.

Here are a few information-gathering questions you should ask when meeting with your customer for the first time:

"How much do you know about our products or services?" (This is a particularly important question if the person you are calling on is new to the position or the industry.)

"How will you use our service?"
"What service are you using now?"

Questions That Identify Problems

This type of question requires some thought before you ask it. You are trying to find out how your product or service could help solve a problem for the customer. Of course, you could simply ask what their biggest problems are right now. But you want to narrow down the inquiry as much as possible. Pretend for a moment that you're a pharmaceutical sales representative selling doctors a newly released asthma medication whose primary advantage is no side effects. Suppose you ask the doctor what his biggest problems are right now. The doctor might say getting paid by the local health plan. Not much help, right? On the other hand, if you say, "Doctor, I know you see a lot of asthma patients. Other physicians have told me that convincing them to take their medication is a problem. Do you have the same experience with asthma patients in your practice?" Notice that to ask this question, you have to do your homework. You have to know that patient compliance is often an issue. You've also verified in advance that the doctor actually treats patients with asthma.

Assuming the doctor agrees, you would then ask the doctor a follow-up question. "How do you handle that problem now?" Chances are that whatever the doctor is currently doing, it's probably frustrating. Thoughtful questioning validates the problem. It also helps focus the customer's attention on the issue.

Questions That Identify Consequences

Once you have uncovered a problem, you must help the customer understand the consequences of not solving the problem now. Again, let's assume the doctor agrees with you. Patients often refuse to take their asthma medication and changing their behavior is difficult. Your follow-up question would be "Do side effects with current medications make it harder for patients to comply?"

Assuming the answer is yes, you could launch into your pitch, telling the doctor that you have a new asthma drug with no known side effects. But you still don't have the doctor's full attention. After all, the doctor already knows all this. Instead, you would ask questions that crystallize the consequences of the problem for the doctor. For example, you could ask:

"Do noncompliant patients take a lot of your time?" or "Are they difficult to satisfy?"

Doctors are extremely busy, yet their earnings are limited by the amount of time available to them. After all, they can only see so many patients in any given day. You've pointed out a problem related to how doctors are forced to use their time in caring for problem patients. At this point, your customer is much more aware of the problem and its implication, and the doctor is almost ready to listen to your proposed solution.

Questions That Suggest Solutions

This type of question is designed to help your customer see how your product or service can help solve the problem you've uncovered. Continuing with our example, you would ask if the doctor would find it beneficial to be able to prescribe an asthma medication with no known side effects. You are still asking a question. A positive response is an invitation to describe the features and benefits of your product. In this scenario, your next question would be "May I tell you about our new prescription drug for asthma?"

The ability to ask good questions relies in good part on what you know. The more you know about your product, your competitors, and your customer's business, the better your questions will be. With more business and life experience, your questions will become even savvier.

Asking solid questions also relies in part on phrasing skills. We are all familiar with courtroom dramas and the type of questions TV lawyers ask. Try to prevent your questions from sounding like a cross examination so you don't badger the customer. If you ask too many leading questions designed to elicit a preferred response, you may get the answers you want but your customers may feel manipulated. Finally, never assume your customer is completely familiar with the foundation of your question. It's rarely productive to ask someone why they aren't using the latest technology available if they've never even heard of it.

Here are eight pointers about asking questions:

1. *Find out how much time the customer has to meet with you.* Although you discussed the time available when you scheduled the appointment, verify your understanding: "I believe we're scheduled for one hour today. Does that still fit your schedule?" Circumstances change. Your buyer might be pressed for time. If you're going to have less time than you thought, adjust your objectives accordingly.

2. *At key points during the meeting, ask if your client's needs are being met.* Ask if you are focusing on the right things. Before transitioning to another topic, be sure to ask if there are any questions on what you just covered.

3. *Be conversational.* The client is not on the witness stand. There's no need to control every minute of the meeting. As with any conversation, subject matter tends to bounce around a bit. Let it.

4. *Take your time.* Don't rush through your questions. Be patient; give your customer time to think before responding.

5. *Use variety in your questions.* It isn't necessary to ask all of your information-gathering questions first. For example, you can intersperse questions that identify problems.

6. *Link questions to the customer's statements.* "You mentioned having difficulty getting paid for that type of service. Would it be helpful if you knew your customer's credit rating in advance?"

7. *Preface questions with statements.* "Last year you bought fifteen percent more of our product than this year. What do you think accounts for the change?"

8. *Don't be afraid to ask the same question more than once.* It often helps to rephrase the question. Don't be surprised if the second response is substantially different from the first. Similarly, if you're not sure you understand the answer to your question, by all means say so. Again, the response may be quite different than what you thought you heard the first time. I'm not sure why this is true, but I have found in many cases that the revised answer tends to be more favorable to my position.

> "I keep six honest serving men
> They taught meall I knew:
> Their names are What and Why and When
> And How and Where and Who."
>
> —Rudyard Kipling

Answering Questions

Here are nine rules for answering questions:

1. Keep your answers short.
2. Take a moment to think before answering.
3. Be honest. If you don't know the answer say so. Offer to get back to them as soon as possible, and then do it. Take a moment to write the question down. It's a reassuring gesture. In my experience I know I have a better chance of getting my question answered if the sales representative writes it down. If they don't, I suspect they will forget.

4. Don't try to be cute. Answer the question they asked.
5. If it's a question you would rather not answer, say so. Simply say something like I am not at liberty to discuss that with you at this time. Then shut up.
6. Look them in the eye when you answer.
7. Repeat or rephrase the question if you are not sure of what they are asking.
8. Resist the temptation to launch into a favorite story or digression that just happens to come to mind. Answer the question first. Follow up with a story if it really adds impact or clarifies your response.
9. Ask them if your response answered their question.

▶*The way you answer questions says a lot about you.*

Overcoming Objections

Objections to the sale keep sales professionals employed. If there were no objections, anybody could sell. Selling truly would be order taking.

"I have these eighteen-inch catheters. They come fifty to a box and ten boxes to a case. They cost one dollar twenty-five per catheter but if you buy six cases, I can let you have them for ninety-five cents each."
"Fine, I'll take twelve cases."

Sure. Sometimes it happens that way but usually there are issues.

"I already have a supplier."
"Your competitor's price is much cheaper."
"Our nurses say your catheters are causing a lot of discomfort for patients."

These objections to the sale tell you "I'm already satisfied with my current supplier. Your price is too high. Your quality is too low." They are typical objections that salespeople hear in all types of business. As you gain experience, you'll develop responses to these objections.

How can you develop a smart communication strategy to deal with obstacles to the sale? First, be sure you really understand the customers' issues. Listen carefully to what they say. Objections tend to fall into one of three categories: misunderstandings, statements of fact, and emotional responses.

Misunderstandings

The customer has the wrong impression of your product or service. Perhaps the customer didn't understand a key element of your presentation.

I was working with the sales team of a health plan owned by physicians and hospitals. The team was having trouble responding to an objection expressed frequently by the employee benefits managers they were calling on.

The benefits managers were afraid that the hospitals and doctors who owned the health plan would have little incentive to control utilization of services and therefore costs. I was told that the benefits managers consistently stated their objection by saying, "That's like the fox guarding the hen house." It's a cliché of course, but, as with all objections, it must be taken seriously.

I suggested to the group that we take the statement literally for a moment. The fox can't be trusted to watch over the hens, because the fox is exactly why the hens must be guarded in the first place. Okay. Does the analogy really work when applied to hospitals and doctors watching over both health care services and health care costs? Do the doctors have an incentive to abuse the system?

Not really, unless they plan to be in the health plan business a very short time. For one thing, the doctors and hospitals had to invest substantial sums to get started. They must also be able to compete with other health plans on quality, cost, and service. Finally, they are professionals who would be risking their reputations and even licenses if they provided health services well beyond the needs of patients. Doctors and hospitals have always had some incentives to provide more rather than less care; that's how they get paid. Owning their own health plan wouldn't necessarily have a significant impact on the way they practiced.

They invested in their own health plan because they had a sincere desire to manage health care in the best interests of their patients while ensuring a reasonable income for their efforts.

In this case, the benefits managers' objection was based on a misunderstanding of the goals and objectives of the doctors and hospitals. Although their concern is understandable, it can be eliminated by a thorough review of the facts.

The more you know about your company's products and services *and* your industry, the better you will be able to handle misunderstandings. Recognize that your task is to change your customer's beliefs. Don't be too eager to point out where they are wrong. Take the time to examine the issue with them. You want to help them reach a new conclusion based on new information.

Statements of Fact

Some objections are factual. The customer has pointed out differences in price, features, or benefits when compared to a competitor's offering. Perhaps your customer needs a feature *no one* can provide at this time.

Acknowledging the verity of the customer's statement is important. This is not the time to be argumentative or to try to minimize the problem. You are there to help the customer achieve his or her goals and solve problems. You have to spend the time to work through the concerns. Probe to find out how important the issue is to the client. Is it really a critical issue or is the customer stalling for some reason? What is the basis for the concern? Is the client expressing an unmet need or a simple preference? Even "facts" aren't always completely objective matters. Maybe your price is higher because you offer a longer warranty or better payment terms.

Sometimes your customer is not the end user but is the buyer representing the actual users. Make sure you ask for permission to talk with the users about the buyer's concerns. You may be surprised to learn that the actual users don't consider the buyer's concerns to be a big problem. Obviously, this is good news, but you must use the information carefully. Tell the buyer what you've learned, offering the information as a different perspective from another source. For example, "Marilyn didn't feel battery size was an issue. Is she missing something important?"

Emotional Responses

The customer is upset about an event or incident in dealing with your firm that was not resolved to their satisfaction. Certainly if the problem hasn't been resolved yet, take care of it immediately.

This type of objection isn't always serious in terms of your product or service itself. Nevertheless, it must be dealt with seriously. While it might be easy to overcome the technical issue, getting at what is actually bothering your customer is your real task. In most cases, it isn't hard to identify this situation if you pay careful attention. Listen to the customer's tone of voice. Note body language and word choices.

Emotion can signal a variety of messages. The customer may be sincerely passionate about solving a problem or identifying a shortcoming. Conversely, an emotional response might be a ploy designed to keep you off balance.

The best way to handle this situation is to hit it head-on. Probing can help you differentiate between legitimate concerns and what might be nothing more than a negotiating strategy. Respond to the objection factually; then gently ask if there is something else bothering the customer. Let the customer know how important it is to you personally to understand any concerns he has. Usually, the customer will open up and express his real concerns.

By analyzing your prospect's objections, you can arrive at a response that should satisfy his concerns. Rather than jump in with a stock answer to an objection you may have heard before, take the time to fully explore the customer's concerns before answering. If you don't fully understand the customer's issues, you probably won't be able to satisfy them, regardless of what you say.

An objection, no matter how serious, is often a sign of interest. Conversely, some customers are reluctant to even express an objection or concern. Sometimes it seems easier to say nothing. In fact, when a customer doesn't express concerns, it might be a sign of trouble. Unless the customer buys your product or signs an agreement during the meeting, you may well be defeated by an unstated objection. What can you do about it? If you suspect there is an unspoken problem, say something like this: "I'm glad you like our product so much. I'm curious though. If you could improve one thing about it, what would that be?" The answer may well reveal any issues that are lurking beneath the surface.

Finally, objections tend to be similar from one client to another. Brainstorming with sales colleagues and other coworkers is a wonderful way to understand and overcome objections. One of your colleagues may have discovered a very effective response to an issue that has you stumped. Working together, your team will nearly always be able to craft a better way to respond to the customer. If you cannot come up with a satisfactory response to a frequently mentioned objection, you've very likely discovered a serious flaw in your product or service.

> *The more you know about your customer,*
> *your company, the competition, and your industry,*
> *the easier it is to handle objections.*

Price Objections

Often, the rubber meets the road when the talk turns to price. If you have been working diligently to build credibility and trust, a discussion about price is your opportunity to cement the relationship. As a buyer, I worry about two things when it comes to price. First, I want to be sure that I'm not paying too much. I have an obligation to my employer to drive the best bargain possible. Second, I don't want to appear to be a weak negotiator.

It's not unlike the feeling most of us get when we buy a new car. We want to feel as though we are really good at driving the price down. The difference for a buyer representing a company is that professional reputation is important to the buyer and the company. Nobody knows what you really paid for your car, but word gets around within the industry about the prices a buyer will negotiate for products and services.

If you understand the buyer's concerns about price, you can communicate more effectively when the inevitable price discussion takes place.

Here are five typical situations:

The customer asks about price too early in the sales process. Perhaps the biggest reason salespeople don't like to discuss price early in a presentation is that they know that price objections are often harder to overcome if the customer doesn't fully understand the value proposition. But customers are sometimes impatient. They want to hear your presentation, but they also want to know the bottom line as soon as possible. Why? There are many reasons. For example, a customer may be wondering if his budget will allow him to make the purchase. He may already have a price from a competitor, and he's eager to see how close you are to matching that price. Perhaps he believes he already knows enough about your service and is ready to talk price.

Regardless of why the customer asks about price, you have to deal with it. As a first step, develop a brief answer that postpones an immediate response. For example, "Can we hold off on that for a while? I want to be sure I've explained our service to your satisfaction before we look at costs."

If customers persist, give them the information they asked for. To do otherwise might plant seeds of doubt. If that happens, they won't be really listening to your presentation anyway. They'll be worrying about the price and what you are trying to hide. In effect, you will be creating an obstacle: Their concerns about you and what you might be up to. If you're dealing with a qualified customer, you'll work out any price concerns.

The customer says, "It's not in my budget." When customers claim they don't have money in their budget, acknowledge the statement; let them know you understand the problem. Be sure to let them know that from your perspective, you are confident that they will put the money in their next budget if they see the value of your product.

Sometimes when a customer says it's not in the budget, it might be her way of telling you that she isn't interested. It's your job to probe and uncover other issues that may be behind the "not in my budget" response. Ask how the budget process works in her organization. Find out when budgets are developed and how the approval process works. This information will help you plan accordingly if you conclude that money really isn't available now.

Be sure you understand which department's budget will be affected by the purchase, as well as where in the budget the money will be applied. For example, if you were selling a consulting service, your fees would likely be allocated to a consulting expense rather than to capital expenditures.

Don't assume that your buyer is thoroughly knowledgeable about how budgets work. It might even be possible for the customer to allocate a portion of the cost to another department if your product and service benefits that department as well.

You bring up price. Knowing that buyers like to feel that they are good negotiators, you will probably quote a price that is a bit higher than what you expect the final price to be. When you have made your presentation and summarized the features and benefits, typically salespeople say something like this. "Here's the good news. You can have this for a very good price. It only costs $755 per unit."

A smart customer says nothing in response, waiting for you to say something else. Other than adding "How does that sound to you?" you resist the temptation to say anything else. You want their reaction. Yet, you may be inviting an objection by opening the discussion as if there is nothing more to talk about. It's presumptuous to claim that your price is good. Whenever I hear that, my antenna goes up immediately. I feel as if I'm being manipulated. The buyer always decides if the price is right.

Is there another way to handle this situation? I think there is. As a customer I would prefer to hear this: "The price is seven hundred and fifty-five dollars per unit. Based on what we've outlined, I believe it's a fair price. Do you have any questions at this point?"

What's the difference between the two approaches? In the latter example, the salesperson demonstrates respect for the buyer and shows confidence in the price without trying to sell the price to the buyer.

Both parties know that there will probably be some negotiation involved. It is silly to think that you have maneuvered to some advantage by telling the customer it *only* costs $755.

Buyers are more sophisticated today than ever. When it's time to discuss price, handle price in a straightforward manner. Your customer will appreciate it.

The customer tells you your price is too high. If you've done your homework, you have a pretty good idea of whether your price is competitive. When a customer says your price is too high, either they already have a better price for what they believe is a comparable product or they're testing your reaction. There are three things you should do upon hearing your price is too high:

1. *Verify that your customer really has a comparable alternative in mind.* If there are meaningful differences between the alternatives, point them out and reassert the fairness of your price. In other words, if your price is where it should be, defend it.

2. *Decide whether you will hold firm or lower your bid.* Recall why you set your price where you did. Was it a strategic bargaining position, or have you set the price at a level you think is fair and reasonable? If you are confident your price is fair, hold your ground. Reiterate your position, letting the customer know this is really your best offer. You will be pleasantly surprised by how often this strategy works, provided you have established credibility with your client.

3. *If you know your price is higher than it needs to be, unless you had a good reason for setting it at that level, you will likely hurt your credibility in the ensuing discussion.* When setting your price, keep in mind that if you must reduce it, there should be a valid explanation for the change. The bigger the drop, the better the explanation must be. If your customer feels as if you highballed him, hoping he wouldn't notice, your relationship is on life support.

Your customer complains that your current price is out of line with new bids. Your customer has been buying from you for several years. He seemed happy, but then he tells you that a competitor has just offered him a better price for the same product. If your immediate response is that you would like an opportunity to rectify that situation, think again. Recently, a sales representative calling on our company said that very thing to me. I was turned off. I felt as though he was aware that his price wasn't competitive. We were paying more than we should be paying, but he wasn't going to offer a price reduction unless he was forced to take action.

Why not spend a few minutes probing the customer to make certain that he is comparing apples to apples? Discuss the current situation; review how and when your current price was established and when it is due for renewal.

With the proper background and setup, you can thank the customer for bringing the issue to your attention and offer to review the matter in detail. Perhaps you can come back to the customer with an alternative that might include other concessions you want in exchange for a lower price. Don't drop your price until you have fully evaluated the situation. Take the time to walk through your analysis with the customer. If you decide a reduction is in order, make sure he understands why you reduced the price.

Also, don't lose sight of the switching costs a customer must contend with if they change vendors. Even though someone may have offered a better price, the internal costs of changing vendors, whether in dollars or extra work, can't be ignored. Sometimes the customer needs a reminder.

▶*Preparation is the price you pay
to get the price you deserve.*

Asking for the Business

Probably millions of words have been written about the art of closing the sale. It is perhaps the most difficult communication in selling. Why do so many salespeople find it so hard to ask for the business? Obviously fear of rejection is one reason. But most salespeople get over that or they get out of sales. The bigger issue is that salespeople may not be sure they have earned the right to ask. In too many cases, the salesperson hasn't laid the proper foundation. They've treated closing as an event rather than a process, and all their training says ask for the order. So they meekly try one of the many closes they've been taught. Or they avoid it altogether and pretend they asked. If you've really done your homework, given the customer everything she's asked for and helped her understand her needs, you have every right to ask her for a commitment.

Today's buyer is much more sophisticated than in times past. Unless you are in retail sales, selling washers and dryers, cars, or suits off the rack, closing techniques such as the "now or never" close or the "Ben Franklin," which fill an immediate need and do not require building a long-term customer relationship, are best forgotten.

If you are selling a product or service that does require building a long-term trusting relationship, traditional closing behaviors don't work on today's more sophisticated customers. If the buyer doesn't really want or need your service, can't afford it, or has a fundamental problem with your product or service that hasn't been adequately addressed, no closing technique is going to work for you. No doubt you've heard stories about a salesperson who manipulated a client into a sale by closing at just the right time. I would wager, though, that there weren't many repeat sales to those customers. Traditional closing techniques tend to be manipulative; experienced buyers are wise to such techniques and likely to be irritated by such ploys.

If you've done your homework, getting the customer to buy from you is a natural conclusion to the sales process. From the outset, you are communicating with your prospects. You're asking questions, learning about their needs, their fears, their budget, and their alternatives. Using what you've learned, you have customized your presentation to fit those needs.

Each client has unique desires and concerns. Understand your client's needs and respond to them, so you can help the client reach the logical conclusion that doing business with you makes sense. Once your customer makes that decision, price becomes less critical.

There is a distinct possibility you don't even have to ask for the business. Your customers will tell you they're ready to buy. It happens when you take the time to communicate—talking, listening, and exchanging ideas while building credibility, which is an extremely important part of that foundation. If you have taken the time to communicate, talk, listen, and build credibility, chances are you won't even have to ask for the business. Your customers will tell you they're ready to buy.

Here are five key communication strategies for closing the sale:

1. *Look for buying signs that suggest the customer is ready to close.* Questions about your price, warranty, and durability often indicate a strong interest.
2. *Keep it simple and be direct.* Ask for the business. Ask firmly and with intent. Don't say, "I was kinda' hopin' you might do business with us." Say instead, "May I do this for you? I think we'll work well together." Your words should convey how much you want to serve your client's needs.
3. *Don't be afraid to ask more than once.* In fact, from the outset, you should let the customer know how much you want to work with him. Don't overdo it, but make

certain that before your meeting is over he can clearly see how much you want his business.

4. *Be confident but not cocky.* The difference between the two lies in respect for your customer. You're not being presumptuous. Rather, you're letting your customer know that you value her business. Whereas a cocky person might say, "Hey, we're the best in the business everybody knows that," a confident person would say, "We have a good track record. We hate to disappoint anybody. We can deliver what you're asking for."

5. *Take the advice of a friend of mine—when you've made the sale, shut up.*

▶*Closing the sale is a process, not an event. The process begins with your first contact.*

When the Meeting Is Over

The meeting is over. You shake hands with the customer and say your goodbyes. Before leaving for your next appointment, you and your colleagues stop in the restroom to freshen up. You wait in the lobby for the elevator and then share the ride with three people you don't know. What do you and your colleague talk about during these minutes? *Anything but the meeting you just finished.* Talk about the weather, where you're going for dinner, or your daughter's recital.

The temptation to rehash the meeting you just completed can be overwhelming. Maybe you're excited about your chances of getting the business. Perhaps you're concerned about something you said and want immediate feedback. Don't give in to this temptation. Your comments may be overheard. You might say something that can be misinterpreted. If it gets back to your customer, it can diminish your bargaining power or even threaten the sale itself. It's not worth the risk. Wait until

70

you're in the car. Then you can get everything off your chest.

▶*Sometimes silence is your best communication strategy.*

Follow Through

I am constantly amazed by how many sales representatives fail to follow up after a sales call. Early in my career, I worked for a man in the health insurance industry who understood this phenomenon perfectly and took full advantage of it. We met with numerous health care providers wanting us to provide insurance coverage for all manner of services, from brain injury rehabilitation to homemaker services.

In many instances, my boss knew that we could not cover such services. Yet, he frequently encouraged these people to put together specific proposals for our review. He was careful to sketch out a few vague clouds that might pour a little rain on our visitors' parade, but generally he was most encouraging.

One day, after one of these meetings, I asked him why he was so optimistic with these people when he knew perfectly well we would never approve their programs. He smiled and said, "It's very unlikely we'll see them again. They won't do the work necessary to get a decent proposal together. Why should I be the heavy? They left happy."

I didn't agree with his tactics, but he had a point. We wouldn't see very many of them again. Only a few were persistent enough to actually send us the information we requested. Occasionally, one of them would hound us sufficiently to persuade us to experiment with their services.

Good follow-up is the essence of effective sales communication in action. Often, it's the difference between success and failure. Once you have made a sales call, if you have even a tiny reason to hope for a sale, create a follow-up plan with the customer before you leave. Tell them what you intend to do next and when you will do it.

When I was selling, I rarely met customers with a proposal in hand. For one thing, I realized that I might need to customize my proposal to address specific needs or concerns. Also, the promise of a proposal gave me a built-in reason to get in touch with the prospect again. Whether you are following up with a phone call, a letter, or additional information, let them know you will take action and then do it. They will be surprised. They will remember you. Following up sends a powerful message. It says you are committed. It says you are reliable. It says you care.

▶*Follow through on your promises and you'll be indispensable.*

Chapter 5

Listening

Your Number One Sales Communication Skill

Studies show that 45 percent of our time is spent listening. Other research indicates that while most of us speak at a rate of about two words per second, we can hear and process more than eight words per second. If you use this extra time to observe tone and body language, you will be better able to grasp the true meaning of the speaker's words. Active listening is hard work, but you can improve your listening skills with practice. Being an active listener gives you a very powerful competitive edge. People tend to like good listeners because listeners are paying attention to them. Active listeners also learn what they need to know about their customers.

All too often today, our conversations are comprised of talking and waiting rather than talking and listening. We wait for the other person to finish talking so we may begin talking again. Although we are taught reading, writing, and even public speaking in school, listening is not always emphasized.

Listening is the most important communication skill a sales professional must have to succeed. In fact, truly successful salespeople will tell you that if you listen closely to your customers they will tell you how to sell to them. They will tell you what is bothering them about your product, their worries, their goals, and their dreams. It takes patience to get this kind of information. You can't get it in a fifteen-minute conversation. First, you must earn your client's trust. Listening in a nonjudgmental manner is a great way to start.

The price of not listening is high. Back when HMOs were high on every health care provider's list of desirable customers, a friend of mine, a regional sales specialist for a large home care company, got an appointment with perhaps the most prestigious HMO in the country. Since my friend had worked in an HMO previously, he understood their concerns. Unfortunately, his local branch manager, who knew very little about HMOs, insisted on joining the call. Rather than talking and listening during the meeting, the manager talked and waited. Because of his impatience and lack of understanding, he interrupted the customer during the meeting, making irrelevant comments. Shaking his head in bewilderment as he told me the story, my friend said, "The woman pretty much dismissed us at that point. She knew perfectly well we weren't really interested in solving her problems. We lost all credibility right then and there." Had the branch manager *listened* instead of waiting for his turn to talk, he might have made a sale.

Here are ten active listening tips:

1. *Find a motivation to listen.* If your doctor walked into the exam room and said, "I have some news for you," would you be all ears? You bet. Whether it's your commission, an opportunity to learn something new, or a chance to make a friend, find a reason to pay attention.
2. *Concentrate.* Make eye contact and hold it (without staring).
3. *Don't let distractions break your concentration.*
4. *Suspend all judgment.* Don't let the other person's dress, appearance, accent, title, or words influence your willingness to listen.

5. *Take notes.* You will be paying your customers a compliment by writing down what they say.

6. *Ask questions.* Asking questions signals that you are engaged in the conversation and interested in your customer's point of view.

7. *Acknowledge that you are listening with reassuring nods.* Say things like "Yes, I understand," "I see," and so on.

8. *Confirm what you heard.* Play it back to the customer. If there are any misunderstandings, now is the time to clear them up.

9. *Focus on tone of voice and body language as much as on words.* Listen for what is not said. Watch for gestures, facial expression, and signs of hesitation. If there is a conflict between the customer's words and body language, the latter is more likely a true expression of the person's feelings.

10. *Resist the temptation to interrupt the customer.* Don't assume you know where the speaker is going. People will often surprise you. Let them.

"Listening well is as powerful a means of communication and influence as to talk well."
—John Marshal

Are They Listening to You?

You're in the middle of an exciting description of the features and benefits of your new service. The prospect is fidgeting. She's shuffling paper. She's not making eye contact. Your prospect isn't listening to you. How do you regain her attention? Stop speaking. In a moment, the customer will notice you aren't talking anymore. Now make and hold eye contact, and begin speaking again. Be subtle about it. This is not the time to show irritation. After all, your prospect might be tired or preoccupied about a problem at home. Usually, a simple pause will regain your listener's attention.

As I mentioned earlier, make sure you aren't speaking in a monotone. Vary the speed of your delivery and show your enthusiasm. If your presentation lacks energy, your listeners will be easily distracted. Maintain eye contact. If you fully engage your listeners, you will have their undivided attention. You can also do this by building a little suspense into your presentation. Let them know that in a few minutes you're going to tell them about the unusual circumstances that led to the founding of your company. Promise to explain how one of your customers discovered a completely different use for your product that no one in your company had ever considered. By being just a little bit creative, you can hold your prospect's attention and get results.

▶ *Give your customers reasons to listen.*

Chapter 6

Nonverbal Communication

Selling Is More Than Words Alone

Research suggests that words account for only a small percentage of the messages we send. At a face-to-face meeting, we communicate

- 7 percent of a message by words
- 38 percent by voice tone
- 55 percent by nonverbal signals

The ability to interpret nonverbal communication is a critical sales communication skill. If you want to increase your chances of success, pay attention to body language. Become acutely aware of surroundings and carefully observe your own behavior as well as the behavior of those around you.

▶*Nonverbal communication is often more important than verbal communication.*

Body Language

Body language—such as facial expression, eye contact, gestures, and posture—plays a key role in the impression we make. We all have an innate sense that allows us to interpret gestures, facial expressions, and postures. We also make judgments about people based upon characteristics such as age, size, what they're wearing, and, in some cases, even ethnic origin or race. While body language and physical characteristics provide important clues about you and your customers, remember that these observations and assumptions are not always accurate.

Researchers have shown that human beings are capable of making more than 7,000 facial expressions. How many can we accurately interpret? A simple gesture, like the crossing of arms, may signal resistance or is it a subconscious effort to hide a protruding belly? Regardless, when a person's words don't match their body language, we are more inclined to believe the body language.

Reading body language is tricky. While it should play a role in your decision-making, be wary of reading too much into any one observation. Learning to read body language takes conscious, sustained effort. You will get better at reading people the more you consciously notice their movements. Your interpretations of what you see will become increasingly accurate.

Become a student of body language, yours and your customer's. Learn to recognize positive and negative nonverbal messages, focusing your own efforts on positive behaviors.

Your Body Language: What to Aim For

- Make good eye contact without staring.
- Avoid sharp eye contact with a colleague when you've heard something either delightful or distressing. Your customer will notice and probably won't like it.
- Stand up straight and sit up straight, but avoid stiffness in either posture or gestures.
- Use warm natural gestures rather than sharp forceful movements.
- Get closer to the customer if the situation permits. Moving in closer so you can both get a better look at your product or a report you are explaining is acceptable. Leaning toward the

other person is usually perceived favorably, provided you don't violate his or her space.

- Body language is contagious. If your body language is positive, the people around you are likely to follow suit. Likewise, if it's negative, people will pick up on that as well.
- Smiles should be natural. A forced smile is easy to detect and can create doubts about your sincerity.

Your Customer's Body Language: What to Look For

- Fidgeting or yawning may be a sign of boredom or impatience.
- If the customer is leaning or moving away even as you move closer, there may be a problem. Perhaps the customer disagrees with your point of view, or simply doesn't trust you. Observe your interaction carefully and if it's appropriate, gently ask if there is an issue that you need to address.
- If the customer frequently interrupts your presentation or is easily distracted, it may be a sign of impatience.
- Facial expressions that suggest disagreement, irritation, or worry should be addressed. Don't ignore them.
- Patterns are more significant than an individual gesture or expression. Just because someone yawns doesn't mean boredom. However, yawning combined with leafing through papers and drumming fingers might be a pretty good indication that you are not getting through to the customer.

When the Body Language Is Negative

When you're getting signals that suggest you are not connecting with the customer, stop what you are doing, pause, and ask if you are meeting their needs. Asking "are we on the right track?" will usually elicit a helpful response.

Let your style dictate your approach to the problem. A friend handled this situation with a prospect he was meeting for the first time by being as straightforward as possible. He was trying to explain his product, but the prospect kept looking at her watch and shuffling papers. He stopped talking. The silence got her attention. Then he said, "You know what? You're busy and I'm busy. So if you really aren't interested in what we have to offer, just say so and I'll be on my way."

Her response was to ask a question about the product, which most likely described her primary objection to the sale. He had a good answer, and the meeting moved forward. Only this time she was an active participant in the discussion. My friend realized what many salespeople don't understand. Any one sales call is rarely critical to your company, your success, or your job. We have only so much time to achieve our goals. Sometimes it takes courage to use your communication skills to help you stay on track. He did not change the tone of his voice to show irritation when he challenged the prospect. He was polite but firm. It worked.

Here's another example:

I was trying to get an appointment with the contracting director of an HMO. This was an important account. It took me four months to get the director of provider contracting to meet with me. When I got there, he made it very clear that he wasn't really interested in contracting with the company I represented. He didn't actually tell me that. When I walked into his office, I could not help noticing that he was playing music. It was loud. Just below the level that would interfere with our ability to hear each other but certainly louder than was polite under the circumstances. Instinctively, I didn't say a word about it. I just proceeded with the agenda I had proposed. He sat there expressionless.

After ten minutes of this, I decided to acknowledge what he obviously believed. I said, "I am painfully aware that your organization can live without us. We need you more than you need us, but I sincerely believe we can make a contribution to your organization's success."

With that, he stood up, walked over to his tape player, and turned it off. Then he said, "I've been waiting to hear somebody from your organization admit that for years." Apparently, one of my predecessors had made the mistake of telling him that he had to sign a high-priced contract. When he refused, the salesperson said, "You need us. You'll be calling me."

Once we set the record straight, the director was ready to listen to my proposition. We had a good meeting. Not only did we sign a contract, we did a lot of business. And, our meetings after that day were cordial.

▶*Become a student of body language. You'll make more sales.*

Look Them in the Eye!

Research shows that eye contact signals a readiness to interact. Without it, whether it's intentional or accidental, the likelihood of interaction is reduced. Other studies suggest that people who engage in high levels of eye contact are seen as more influential and effective in their relationships with others. Eye contact tends to go down when people talk about something difficult or embarrassing or when they're trying to hide something.

Making eye contact helps get and hold your listener's attention. With a little practice, you will learn to use eye contact to detect whether your message is getting through or you are losing someone's interest.

How much eye contact is good? Studies show that people look at each other 50 to 60 percent of the time they talk, although the person doing the talking averages 40 percent while the listener averages 70 percent. I think most of us have an innate sense of what is appropriate. We know the difference between engaging someone and staring at them. Eye contact is an essential nonverbal resource in your communication arsenal.

▶*Making eye contact strengthens your message.*

That Personal Touch

A recent Cornell University study revealed that tips increased by 29 percent for waiters who touched their customers. Touching is of course a very intimate and powerful form of communication. A pat on the back or touching the customer's arm as you make a key point shows warmth. Try it. Just be sure to keep it within the bounds of socially acceptable behavior. Most of us accept touching as a sign of warmth. If you sense someone stiffening, it's best to back off.

▶*Touching is a sign of warmth and caring.*

Dress for Success

The rules have changed when it comes to appropriate dress for a sales call. Once it was standard to wear a suit and tie or a dress. Today business casual dress is common. As a result, it's no longer necessary to wear a business suit to call on your customer if their office dress policy is business casual. Of course, if you are more comfortable in business attire, by all means dress up. A business suit is rarely out of place. If you are comfortable in business casual dress, keep in mind that the definition of business casual varies from one business to another. Chances are good that in the course of a day, you will run into a variety of dress policies. If you keep in mind that what you are wearing is a form of communication, it shouldn't be a problem.

- Some rules never change. Whatever you're wearing, it must be neat and clean. Clothing shouldn't look worn-out, be wrinkled, or have stains. Shoes must be polished. Keep your wardrobe fresh and flexible.

- Although business casual may permit a wide variety of choices in clothing or color, you may want to stay with basic colors and time-honored styles. Don't allow what you're wearing to be a distraction. This includes jewelry by the way. Think twice before wearing obviously expensive rings, bracelets, or other flashy items. Your customers will notice these things. They might resent your apparent success. Unless your industry expects that kind of thing, you are probably better off leaving the good stuff home.
- If you aren't sure about dress code, ask when you schedule the appointment. If you arrive out of sync (i.e., you're in a business suit and they're not or vice versa), comment on it if your instincts tell you to do so. Use a light touch. Self-deprecating humor works well. If you feel you must apologize, make it brief and move on.
- Unless it is your intention, be careful not to signal your agenda by what you are wearing. Everyday business casual dress has made formal business attire a symbol of seriousness. If you meet with your customer regularly in business casual attire, should you wear a suit when it's time to negotiate a new agreement? On the other hand, does your customer's dress suggest anything about how important they think this meeting is?
- Look closely at the way your customers dress. It might tell you something about the way they feel about themselves, their moods, and their expectations.

▶*What you are wearing creates an immediate impression.*
Dress with that in mind.

Twitches, Quirks, and Fidgets

We all have an idiosyncrasy or two that we could do without. Usually we are completely unaware of them. When you were a child, your parents probably told you to stop fidgeting or maybe asked why you were sitting there with your mouth open, staring into space. If we're lucky, we correct most of these little problems by the time we reach adulthood. Still, we all have something we need to work on. A simple twitch, a fidget, a meaningless sound, or even certain words can be very distracting to your listeners.

When such mannerisms carry over to adulthood, they can be particularly troublesome. Rarely will someone mention it to you. No matter how distracting your behavior may be, most people will observe in silence. There are exceptions of course. I had a boss once who was kind enough to tell me that I had a habit of drumming my fingers on the table during meetings. He said he could always tell when I was bored because I would go into my little drummer boy routine. He was right, and I worked hard to eliminate that particular behavior. As we all know, criticism is often hard to swallow. That's why people hesitate to mention these things.

Still, handicapping yourself with a distracting mannerism is counterproductive. Some mannerisms suggest nervousness or uncertainty. Constantly clearing your throat or wringing your hands are examples. Other behaviors such as foot tapping and the aforementioned finger drumming might suggest boredom or impatience.

In sales you fight hard every day to earn the confidence of your customers. One of your goals is to be seen as an equal in each transaction. If you want to be taken seriously, identify your distracting behavior and eliminate it. Start by asking those closest to you if they notice anything about your manner that is distracting. It could be anything from a twitch to the frequent and repetitive use of certain words. Don't take their observations to heart. Remember you asked for the feedback. Ask several people from different areas of your life, including business and social acquaintances. Once you are aware of the problem, you can fix it. Be patient with yourself. Chances are you've been doing it for a while. You'll probably slip from time to time, but you will overcome it if you persist.

▶*Don't let distracting mannerisms weaken your message.*

Office Surroundings

Sales calls are frequently conducted in conference rooms. After waiting in the reception area, you are escorted to a conference room where the meeting will be held. Although the reception area and the conference room may provide useful clues about the company you are calling on, the opportunity to meet your customer in his or her office can give you considerably more insight.

Many people surround themselves with reminders of why they work so hard. Offices are filled with clues that reveal how your customers see themselves. Let your eyes sweep the room, taking in family photos, works of art, plaques, and trophies or hobby-related items like golf paraphernalia. Every object could be a story begging to be told. Each story contains seeds from which sprout insights that reveal potential areas of common ground between you and your customer. Since productive relationships often begin by finding common ground, never miss an opportunity to observe your customer's office and comment on what you see. Ask questions, demonstrating genuine interest in the other person.

In my office I keep a Louisville Slugger baseball bat. People almost always notice it. I have been asked in a good-natured way if I use the bat to beat vendors into submission. Actually, the bat is there as a personal memento.

My name is inscribed on the bat. It was part of a sales campaign I conducted several years ago for the company I work for now in an entirely different capacity. Someone who asks about the bat will learn that I was once in their shoes, calling on purchasers. To me, that's a good example of common ground.

Making observations and engaging in conversation about your customer's office surroundings can indeed be revealing. I will never forget traveling nearly 1,000 miles to call on an HMO executive who had a picture of two lovely little girls on his desk. The locally based sales representative I was working with said something to the executive about how pretty the girls were. He responded by saying without a trace of humor, "Them? Tax deductions. That's all they are. What can I do for you today?" Obviously he wanted to portray a tough guy image. He was combative and determined to be unreasonable. It was a difficult meeting. We weren't surprised after his initial comments.

You may also be able to gain additional insights about your client by observing other factors. Is the office large or small? Where is it located relative to other workers? Is the office so neat that paper clips are arranged according to size and color? Is it filled with memorabilia from college days? Is there a row of half-filled coffee cups sitting on memos ringed with coffee stains?

Information like this can help you understand the customer. Naturally, appearances can be misleading. Don't jump to any conclusions based on what you see. On the other hand, don't entirely discount them.

▶*A person's office is a conversation piece*
filled with clues about who they are.

Chapter 7

Written Communication

A Few Writing Basics

Don't be discouraged if writing doesn't come easily for you. Even professional writers have problems that can seem insurmountable. Having to complete sales reports, send letters to customers, or complete requests-for-proposal forms with dozens of questions can be an overwhelming task for the sales professional.

Generally sales professionals crave interaction and prefer working with other people. Writing is a solitary act. Yet, there will be times when you must put your thoughts in writing. As you work your way up in your organization, you will be expected to express yourself in writing even more. The most important thing to remember is that you don't have to be an Ernest Hemingway or a Peggy Noonan to write so you can be understood. There are a few basic rules you can follow to improve your writing. As with everything worth doing, it takes some practice.

Five Ideas to Get You Started

1. *Organization is the key to writing a message that your readers will understand.* It is always wise to start with an outline to better organize your thoughts. If you're struggling with an outline, don't worry about it. Take a blank piece of paper and write your thoughts about the

subject as they occur to you. It might be a single word or a sentence fragment. Just get it all down on paper. When you're finished, review what you've written and number each item in the order of its importance to your message. You now have an outline. I can't stress enough the importance of organizing your material. If your correspondence is unorganized, your readers won't understand your thoughts and may not bother to read what you've written.

Remember that written messages, like presentations, have three distinct parts, each serving a specific function. Every letter should have an opening, a body, and a close, or, to put it another way, a beginning, a middle, and an ending. The beginning tells your readers why you are writing to them. The middle provides support via facts, statistics, anecdotes, quotes, or other useful bits of information that support your position or request. The ending briefly summarizes your position and asks the reader to take a specific action.

2. *Professional writers will tell you that writing is rewriting.* *Sales Talk* went through many drafts before you saw it. Although you will rarely have time to complete multiple drafts before you send a business letter, it can always be improved by some editing. When you complete your first draft, put it away and let it breathe on its own for a while. Sleep on it if you're not pressed for time, but even fifteen minutes will help. When you return to your work, read through it for clarity. I'll bet you'll find a few areas you can improve.

3. *Find a friendly editor.* Ask someone you trust to read your material. If there are sections they don't understand, do some more editing. If you're using Microsoft Word, grammar and spelling errors should not be a problem. However, don't rely exclusively on Word.

Sometimes you will have a reason for a particular spelling or structure. Oftentimes, the computer does not understand what you are trying to convey and will put in wrong corrections. And, Microsoft Word won't correct words used improperly but spelled correctly.

4. *Use a thesaurus.* It will help you find the best word to express your ideas. It will also add some variety to your language, which keeps people reading.

5. *Buy and read a good book on writing.* You can't beat *The Elements of Style* by E. B. White.

"The secret of all good writing is sound judgment."
—Horace

When to Write a Letter

Letter writing is a dying art form. In business it may be dead already. E-mail, which is covered in Chapter 8, is a much less formal and quicker way to disseminate information. Still, the written letter continues to be a very powerful form of communication in sales. The very fact that letters are used so infrequently makes them unique today. Done properly, a letter is a creative way to get someone's attention. Here are a few suggestions about letter writing that will help you get results.

To Introduce Yourself

A personal letter telling new customers about you can help break the ice. Emphasize your desire to be helpful and your commitment to satisfy their needs. Mention your credentials. If you are new to the company, tell them why you took the job. If you know something about the customer's company (and I hope you do), mention that as well. If your firms have been doing business, acknowledge it, expressing appreciation for the relationship. Promise to continue to build on what has been accomplished. If there were issues that interrupted the relationship, pledge to fix what went wrong.

To Document Promises

During a sales call you will, from time to time, offer to do something for your client. It may be gathering more information about the product or service, special pricing, a product sample, or a copy of an article. Over time, I've found that many salespeople tend to be a bit vague about promises. If you want to bowl your customer over, try sending a letter that day or the next, confirming what you promised and when they can expect it. Even better, include the requested items with your letter.

Believe me, you will be remembered. It will put you in the minority of those who always deliver what they promise.

To Outline Terms

You've negotiated the deal. Now you're ready to celebrate. Go ahead; you earned it. But before you toast your hard work and good fortune, draft a letter confirming the deal. Keep the letter short.

Thank your customers for their business and briefly outline the terms. Congratulate them if it's appropriate. Don't add anything that you haven't already agreed upon. The written document makes the deal very real in the customer's mind.

If there is a misunderstanding, your letter will make it apparent right away. I know some people might feel that there is an element of risk involved in sending the letter. What if you say something that *creates* a new objection? I think this is unlikely if you have done a good job during the sales process. Regardless, if there is a problem, it will surface either when you are trying to get a contract signed or during the implementation. Who needs that? The sooner you uncover an issue, the better your chances of resolving it. A letter outlining the terms shows confidence in yourself, your product, and your customer.

▶ *Write a letter when you have something important to say.*

Letters People Will Read

Although business letter writing is a declining art, most of us still receive form letters. Such letters usually go on (and on) to tell the recipients all about an opportunity they can't afford to pass up. We're just as likely to get them at home as we are at work. We are all tired of these letters. Most of us barely glance at them. More often than not, we toss them in the wastebasket without opening them.

The fact is, any letter you send will be competing with all the other mail your customer gets, including e-mail. Here are some examples of letters that beg to be read.

Handwritten Letters

I always read a handwritten letter. They are rare and irresistible. Just make sure your handwriting is legible. Of course sales professionals rarely have enough time to handwrite letters. But adding a handwritten note to a typed letter is the next best thing. I am also more likely to open a letter if my name and address are handwritten on the envelope. If you want customers to read your letters, add a personal touch.

Short Letters

The longer the letter is, the less inclined I am to read it. Experience has taught me that long letters are usually long because the writer didn't spend enough time editing, resulting in a letter long on generalities and short on specifics.

A short letter gets right to the point. It permits the reader to move on to other things. If they need more information, you can be sure that they'll ask you for it.

A Unique First Sentence

Most letters start off with something like, "I am writing to
. . . " or "It was a pleasure to . . . ."

Those openings are so familiar that readers are not
expecting anything unique to follow. On the other hand, Mark
H. McCormack in his book *On Communicating* pointed out
that he would feel compelled to read on if a letter started with
a sentence like, "I want to sell you . . . " or "You are wrong
about . . . ." A first sentence that really grabs your customers'
attention will keep them reading.

A Letter That's Expected

Occasionally, I get calls from sales representatives telling me
they are sending me something in the mail. I would be more
likely to look for it and read it if they said, "I am sending you a
letter. You should have it by tomorrow. I'll call later in the week
to see if you have any questions." Sending me "something" in
the mail is too vague. A letter is specific. Adding a little pressure
by letting me know that I may be quizzed on the letter will probably get me to read it. I'd feel a bit more obligated than if the
letter just arrives on my desk.

We Have a Relationship

Your reputation and standing with your customer has an
impact on how seriously they will take mail they receive from
you. It would feel rude not to read something you sent your customer if you have been doing business together for a while.
Regular correspondence filled with helpful insights about your
client's business or profession are always welcome.

▶*A good letter can do a lot of heavy lifting for you.*

Responding to a Request for Proposal

Occasionally, customers will decide to put their business out to bid. Sometimes they'll send out a request for proposal (RFP) to vendors they believe can provide the products or services they need. Once you decide to respond to the RFP, there are several steps to follow that can improve your chances of being the winning bidder.

1. When you receive the document, review it carefully and write down any questions you have about it. Be sure to call and ask the prospect a few questions about the RFP. If you don't have a few good questions to ask, you aren't trying hard enough.

2. Usually there will be at least some ambiguity in the questions. You need clarification. You also want to personalize the process, even if it's only a little bit, by having a conversation with the person who will review your responses to the RFP.

3. It doesn't hurt to let the reviewer know that you are impressed with the quality of the RFP document itself, assuming that you sincerely believe it was well prepared. In most cases, a great deal of thought and effort was put into developing the RFP. That fact is rarely acknowledged. It also doesn't hurt to sympathize with the reviewer who will have the difficult task of reviewing the responses and making some tough decisions. It's a tough job. Don't overdo it, but help the reviewer to remember you so he or she isn't just looking at a thick three-ring binder when your response arrives.

4. Provide a thorough response to each question. By all means, follow the instructions. If your response to one of the questions will expose a weak spot in your product or organization, don't be tempted to fudge

your answer. Reviewers will quickly spot any attempt to gloss over areas with vague responses. It's not worth it. Chances are your competition has a few weaknesses too. Let the customer sort it out. Your weakness probably won't hurt your chances as much as you might imagine. Simply state the facts. If it's appropriate, include information about your company's plans to address any shortcomings. If you have any doubts, contact the sender for further clarification. Make a special effort to submit a response that looks professional in every respect, including the cover, binding, and graphics. A meticulous RFP response will set you apart from your competition.

5. Finally, be sure to request the opportunity to review your RFP response in person with the customer. Only in a face-to-face meeting can you be sure that they have everything they need to make a good decision. If you are granted a meeting in this situation, give it everything you have. Your message must be absolutely clear: We want your business and we are prepared to earn it.

▶*RFP's are cold and impersonal.*
Warm them up with a personal touch.

Business Reports

The demand for information never stops. Expectations for quick and reliable information increase daily. Yet, in my experience, business reports are fraught with opportunities for misadventure. Only modest commitments should be made in a business report. Surprise your client with something better than they expected.

When your customer asks for reports that deal in numbers, such as the number of items purchased this quarter, price of

94

each item, or total costs, the first question you should ask is what the customer plans to do with the report. You have a much better chance of giving your customers useful information if you know in advance what they are trying to accomplish. Take some time to probe. Sometimes customers don't know for certain what they're looking for. Occasionally, a customer will make a specific request for information you can't provide. By probing to understand their concerns, you may discover that what you *can* provide is sufficient to satisfy their real needs.

Unless the request is routine, discuss the project with the person in your office who will actually have to produce the report before you commit to a delivery date. Consider developing a mockup of the report's format so you can review it with your customers before giving them the finished product.

Beware of creating problems by providing too much information. I can't overemphasize this point: Too much information is not communication. It is, however, a terrific way to create paralysis in decision-making, slowing down the sales process if not derailing it. Before you inundate your customer with reports, touting your ability to sort the data fifty-three ways, carefully consider the impact of all that data. Is the information you are about to provide moving the sale along? Is the data growing the relationship or suffocating it?

A good business report will include these items:

- The date the report was prepared
- A heading describing the nature of the report, including your company name, the name of your customer's company, the items covered, and the time period—such as

Crescent Computers Inc., Personal Computer Purchases by Osborn Inc., Northeastern Region, First Quarter, 2001

- A heading for each column (If the report is more than one page, repeat the column headers on each succceding page.)
- A definition of each term, along with an explanation of abbreviations (For example, if "Quantity Purchased" means items bought less returns, say so.)

Be sure that the report is printed in a font size that is large enough to read easily. If customers ask for a report that, when produced, will be the size of Wyoming, by all means, give them advance warning. You're doing your customers a favor by letting them know that the report they're requesting is likely to be unmanageable. Chances are, they will reconsider the request and shoot for something more reasonable. Your information systems staff will thank you.

▶*Informative, user-friendly reports give you a competitive edge.*

Literacy Rates

Let's close the section on written communication with a few words about literacy rates. The average American today reads between the eighth- and ninth-grade level. Keeping your correspondence simple increases your chances of being understood. Why is this important? The National Adult Literacy Survey ranks people on five literacy levels with each level roughly equivalent to four years of education. Someone reading at level one has the skills needed in the fourth grade. Level three would correspond to the abilities required of a high school graduate.

National Adult Literacy Survey studies suggest that 15 percent of adults holding baccalaureate degrees read prose at levels one or two. Fully 19 percent read documents at those levels. Keep this in mind when you put together proposals, reports, and marketing brochures.

Writing at a level beyond the typical range of your audience is just wasted paper. If you prepare your documents using Microsoft Word, you can check your document for readability based on grade level. For example, a score of 8.0 means that an eighth grader can read the document. Most documents should be written to score between 7.0 and 8.0.

▶*Consider literacy rates in everything you write.*

Chapter 8

The Medium Affects the Message

The Telephone

The telephone is probably the single best communication device in the sales professional's arsenal. Everyone has a phone at their disposal. If you try enough times, you will eventually reach your customer. Whether it's to introduce yourself, schedule an appointment, or provide critical information to move the sale along, a phone call is always an option.

Of course, even the novice salesperson quickly realizes that getting someone on the phone can be about as easy as driving a nail through a two-by-four with cooked spaghetti.

Voice mail has made it a lot easier to avoid taking calls. Most of us have gotten used to leaving messages when no one answers. Not too many years ago, secretaries handled the chore of keeping salespeople away from their targets. A secretary might have mercy on you and let you actually speak to your prospect once in a while; now voice mail has taken over this chore, making it easier to ignore the calls customers would rather not deal with.

Don't take it personally when customers don't take your call. They might be in meetings, or in the middle of reviewing proposals. Most buyers will get back to you if you give them a good reason to do so. Then too, customers are probably less likely to return calls when the caller hasn't clearly enunciated his name or rattled off his phone number at warp speed.

The telephone as a communication medium is distinctly different from face-to-face meetings and often not as effective. Customers have no way of knowing your location. You could be in a hotel room, your bedroom, or their competitor's waiting room. You could be in a three-piece suit, a bathing suit, or your pajamas. On the other hand, you placed the call to the customer's office. Even if you've never seen it, you have a pretty good idea of the surroundings. You don't know if you really have the buyer's attention or what they were doing before they picked up the phone. Asking if it is a good time to talk is more than polite. If the customer is preoccupied, your message isn't as likely to be heard. Be sure you have your listener's attention before you launch into your topic.

When you're on the phone, the communication tools you have available to you are limited to the words and the tone and quality of voice. By all means, use your voice to its maximum effect. Remember, the customer can sense your mood, so project energy and enthusiasm when you speak, regardless of the circumstances.

Customers don't know your desk is a mess, your car payment is overdue, or your dog needs a bath. Unless there is a unique advantage to revealing any of that information, don't tell them. Let customers place you hard at work at your desk in their mind's eye.

Listen carefully for signals customers might send with their voice or with sounds that suggest a particular state of mind. The constant sound of papers rustling, for example, is an obvious tip-off that you don't have your customer's full attention.

Make the Phone Work for You

The following are four suggestions that will help you make the most of your telephone calls.

1. *Set up meetings.* The phone works best when used as a tool to set up a face-to-face meeting. Do your best to speak directly to the person you want to meet. Getting them to pick up the phone isn't always easy; try reaching them in the early morning, early evening, or at lunchtime. Everyone has a routine. Some people like to get to work early. Others prefer to work late. Find out what your customer's routine is. Although secretaries may not take calls for the boss as often as they did in the past, they are still providing other types of support. Get the secretary's name and call that person. Secretaries can help you figure out the best time to call.

2. *Introduce yourself.* Once you get your prospect on the phone, keep it brief. Resist the temptation to sell over the phone. Introduce yourself, tell whom you represent and why you would like to set up a meeting. Ask for an appointment. If the prospect has questions, try to keep your answers brief. Explain that you will cover the material in question in detail when you meet.

3. *Save time.* The phone is a great timesaver when you need to provide additional information or to clarify key points about your product or service. Occasionally, customers will call you requesting information. Unless you are confident you can answer the questions immediately, ask if you can return the call after you have had some time to look into the inquiry.

4. *Grow relationships.* Since the amount of time available to spend in the customer's presence is limited, the phone is a good way to grow the relationship. Your goal is to have the customer recognize you as a valuable professional resource and a reliable friend. A national accounts director at a major medical equipment manufacturer put it this way: "Never call without a reason. Always have

some new information, industry news, or an observation you thought might be helpful to the customer."

Since you can't see each other, your prospects may tend to let their hair down a bit once they begin to get comfortable with you. Obviously, you should avoid certain highly personal topics. There is a big difference between revealing something about yourself and providing intimate details about your personal life. A good guideline to follow might be to ask yourself whether you would reveal this confidence if your boss was also on the line.

Ten Telephone Tips
1. Know your objective in placing the call
2. Identify yourself clearly
3. Sit up straight or stand (Although they can't see you, customers can sense your energy level.)
4. Be conversational
5. Have a script if you are introducing something new or learning to make cold calls to get an appointment
6. Never assume the listener is familiar with your product or your company; ask them
7. Your voice is a key telephone asset. Tape yourself on a few calls to get a handle on how you sound to others. Assess tone, volume, rate of speech, how well you articulate your words, and the clarity of your thoughts.
8. Pause between key points to give them time to absorb what you just said
9. Keep the background noise down
10. Check to be sure they are following you (Ask questions like, "Am I going in the right direction?")

Four Telephone No-No's
1. Don't eat, drink, or chew gum
2. Don't weaken your message with qualifiers (e.g., I'm

just calling to introduce myself or I know you're very busy but . . .)

3. Don't put people on hold to take another call unless you warn them in advance it might happen for a specific and important reason

4. Don't make calls in places where background noises will create a distraction

> ▶*The telephone is a terrific sales tool.*
> *Don't be tempted to take it for granted.*

Voice Mail

Voice mail may be the worst technical advance in communication of all time. When used strictly as a tool to let someone know you've called and that you need to speak with them, it serves a useful purpose. Too often though it is misused to the irritation of the recipient and to the detriment of the sender. Voice mail messages tend to be too long. When you leave a voice mail message, keep it short. There's nothing more irritating than a lengthy voice mail message that meanders like a river.

Listed below are two messages I received not long ago. I have changed the names and some of the circumstances; otherwise, these are verbatim transcripts. The first message was from a supplier with whom our company does millions of dollars' worth of business annually. The caller was asked by the president of his company to contact me to discuss their e-commerce offering. I have tried to capture the flow as closely as possible. That's why there isn't much punctuation. It was spoken as one long sentence. Try reading it out loud.

> *Yeah Len a, this is Martin Barnes with Certified Medical, uhm got a message from Sandy Shelborne, uhm talking about a discussion you guys had uhm not sure it*

was early this week or last week anyway he said maybe I could uhm, uhm be of some help at least talking through a . . . what we're doing from an e-business perspective, uhm we're very interested in working more closely a . . . with our buying partners on improving, uhm our efficiencies and I think have developed pretty strong competency with our online site we have kind of created a scenario where everything that, uhm every a function we can do internally that our customer service can perform, our customers can do on the web so I'd be interested in what you guys a . . . have going and we can go from there. My phone number is area code (155) 555-1234 and again my name is Martin Barnes, uh thanks.

The message was seventy seconds long! The gentleman was actually very intelligent—I spoke with him later and he was very helpful. However, his lack of preparation did not make a good first impression.

The second call came from a sales representative from a company we were not doing business with. As you read through his message, which was eighty seconds long, see if you can spot a few errors in his approach.

Yeah Len good afternoon a . . . my name is Jim Jackson. I'm with Stephens Medical we're a medical device manufacturer a . . . and we have a developed a new infusion system for chemotherapy that I have spoken to some of you're a . . . branch a people about, uhm specifically Mary Miller up in Watertown New York and a . . . there is an interest level in this product it's a product that a . . . delivers the therapy in the sterile flow through sequence a . . . with one patient connection so a . . . it does it automatically and so you don't need to train the patient how to, uhm flush their tubing which is

*a real labor-saving component and I wanted to intro-
duce myself first of all but also find out from you a . . .
what is the best way to go about introducing a new
product like this to, uhm your company's locations from
the corporate level so if you could give me a call sometime I would appreciate it my number is (333) 555-
5678. That is my office number here in Detroit. If I'm
not in just leave a voice mail and also we will be
attending both the HHA show and the HIAC show so if
any of your corporate personnel are going to be at any
of those shows we would love to get together with you
there. Thank you very much for your help. So long.*

This poor guy wasn't well prepared either. Worse, he tried
to sell the features and benefits of his product without knowing
how much I knew about medical terms. He used very specific
technical terms and a couple of acronyms.

Could he have done a bit more research at one of our local
sites to find out how purchasing decisions are made? Certainly.
Our branch locations know the process well and could easily
have explained it to him. He asked me to call him "sometime."
We are all busy people. Nothing he said would create a sense of
urgency for me to return his call. If the caller had simply stated
that the purpose of his call was to set up a meeting to introduce
me to his firm's new infusion system, mentioning that Mary
Miller asked him to call me, I would have promptly returned his
call and agreed to meet with him.

Did you notice that both callers started their message with
"Yeah, Len"? "Hello, Len" is a standard greeting—familiar
without being presumptuous. Don't risk irritating your customer with an off-handed salutation.

Voice mail messages come in two varieties. The messages we
deliberately send and the other type that we send when the
person we're trying to reach doesn't answer the phone. In either

case, if you feel you are unprepared to articulate a concise message, you are probably better off not leaving a message at all.

When you must leave a voice mail message, ask yourself three questions before placing the call:

1. What is my objective in placing the call?
2. Can I achieve it in this voice mail?
3. Will it take me more than twenty seconds to make my point?

If you are satisfied that you can achieve your objective, jot down the key points you need to cover and then mentally rehearse what you plan to say. Remember if you make a mistake, you don't get to do it over again.

Putting a little intrigue into your message can also be a plus. Some people are better at this than others. I have a friend who never asks me just to return her call. She always says something like, "Call me, I need your help with something." Other times she might say, "I learned something interesting today. Call me and I'll tell you about it." Her tone of voice suggests urgency, and I always promptly return her calls.

When you leave your phone number, deliberately slow down. Try to picture the other person writing it down. Give them time to grab a pen and find a piece of paper. It's also a good idea to repeat your number.

Consider your location when placing the call. Are there ambient background noises? Are you calling from a restaurant? If you're calling from home, are your children fighting in the background? You might be sending an unintended message.

A few words about the message you have on your own voice mail system:

- Keep it short
- State your name and title
- Promise to return the call as soon as possible

If your company's voice mail system has a feature that permits callers to bypass your greeting, consider saying so at the start of your message.

> ▶ *To use voice mail effectively,*
> *prepare your thoughts in advance.*

Cell Phones

Cell phones have become indispensable for sales professionals, offering all the advantages of telephones plus easy access to the Internet and lots more. Cell phones make it possible for you to be incredibly responsive to your customers.

You can increase your total productive time available by making calls while traveling from one appointment to the next. If you make calls while driving though, please use headphones and avoid dialing while your vehicle is moving.

However, cell phones come with a built-in trouble spot. Active lifestyles and advances in technology have made people more impatient that ever. We expect instant access to information. When customers demand quick responses, sales professionals are eager and able to please. Unfortunately, information gathered in haste risks inaccuracy. Before you grab that cell phone so conveniently placed on your armrest, make sure you are really prepared to address your customer's needs at that moment.

Once you're engaged in conversation, it may take on a life of its own or take an unexpected turn. Suppose you realize you should be taking notes? At sixty miles an hour in heavy traffic, that can be a problem. It pays to consider your surroundings before jumping on the phone. Just because the technology exists doesn't mean you are required to use it. Immediacy isn't always your ally.

Cell phones also provide a unique temptation to be rude.

Phones frequently ring in the middle of meetings these days, interrupting the discussion.

Turn off your cell phone and pager the minute you get out of your car at the customer's location. That way there's no risk of bad manners. A friend of mine had a particularly embarrassing situation involving his cell phone not long ago. His cell phone was turned on and hidden in the pocket of his suit jacket. He was presenting in front of fifty hospital executives. One of his more emphatic gestures engaged the send button, automatically placing a call. While he was talking, he, along with a good part of his audience, could distinctly hear someone saying, "Hello, HELLO . . . "

Technology.

▶ *The cell phone is a great time saver if used thoughtfully.*

Conference Calls

The conference call can be a very tempting alternative to a face-to-face sales call. It looks particularly attractive when you have an established relationship with the client. Perhaps your schedule is already full and you're thinking you can save a bundle in airfares. The problem is, conference calls in sales situations often don't work because they can be a difficult communication medium.

Let's look at what obstacles you may have in a conference call setup. Sometimes you're dealing with different time zones. You're fresh as a daisy and their day is winding down. You can't see each other. You may be making what you think is a critical point just when a key listener is distracted by an assistant who needs to see him for a moment. If he hits the mute button on his phone, he could be engaged in an entirely different conversation and you wouldn't know it.

I've also noticed that people feel a bit less obligated to "show up" for a conference call. Yet once everyone who kept the appointment is on the line, most of us feel obligated to go ahead with the call in spite of the possibility that a key person might be one of the no-shows. Misunderstandings, especially if tempers flare, can be unbelievably hard to clear up over the phone, with so many people talking at once and no way to effectively referee.

If a situation demands a conference call, there are a few guidelines you can follow that will help you make the most of it.

- Conference calls work best when your objective is simply to disseminate facts. Avoid a conference call if you are using it to introduce a new concept, trying to build consensus, or resolve an issue.
- Clearly state the purpose of the call. Have an agenda ahead of time, preferably a short one.
- Don't invite anybody who doesn't absolutely have to be there.
- Establish a clear leader for the call.
- An hour or so before the appointed time, call each participant to confirm availability. That way if a key participant is not going to be available you still have the option to reschedule the call.
- Set a time limit for the call and stick to it.
- Take a moment to let participants introduce themselves. Ask them to say a few words beyond their name so you can become familiar with different voices. As they introduce themselves, write down their names and titles. If there are more than four people on the call, you may want to ask the participants to identify themselves whenever they speak.
- If the call starts to go awry, don't hesitate to pull the plug and suggest a face-to-face meeting at everyone's earliest convenience. Do this before you find yourself having to do damage control.
- Follow up the call with minutes of the meeting to ensure there are no misunderstandings.

▶ *Conference calls have limited applications in sales situations.*

Video Conferencing

Video conferencing is still relatively new to business and isn't being used routinely yet in most business settings. Still, with communication satellites circling the earth and broadband eventually making the Internet hospitable to video, most of us will likely participate in a videoconference some time in the future.

While the videoconference isn't likely to replace face-to-face meetings, it will certainly supplement them. As a participant, you need to be acutely aware that this medium can have a significant impact on your success or failure. Think of it as a conference call with pictures. You will be on television. Perhaps you won't be in front of millions, but you will be in front of people who really matter to you.

Customers, executives, and coworkers will watch you perform in a medium where we have all grown used to seeing perfection. Dan Rather, Diane Sawyer, and Bryant Gumbel don't make many mistakes. They don't fidget, look bored, and doodle on notepads or gesture wildly to make a point. That is the standard by which you will be measured. After a lifetime of watching television, we're used to seeing professional communicators. It's what we expect.

The teleconference gives you new communication issues to think about. Being aware of the medium will help you monitor your behavior. If you really were appearing on a network broadcast, you would be completely focused on the event, concerned about your appearance as well as your words.

Although it might be some time before you or your company participates in a teleconference, you can begin to prepare for the event by making it a point to notice the way professionals on news and talk shows behave. How do they dress? Watch closely for gestures. You'll notice that gestures are confined to head movements and facial expressions to emphasize key points. That's because forceful hand gestures can be misinterpreted when seen on TV. They don't translate the same as they do in person. Also, most shots tend to be close-ups so that hands are not even seen. What are they wearing? Do differences in style of dress or color selection seem to influence your perceptions? You can also learn a great deal from TV veterans about the importance of pace, tone of voice, and word selection.

Eventually, you will recognize certain commonalities in the way the pros handle television. It might not be a bad idea to emulate them when your turn comes.

> ▶*A videoconference is a performance*
> *even if you are just sitting in the room.*

E-Mail

It's easy to take e-mail for granted. Yet, e-mail isn't just the latest in a long line of communication enhancements. From the posted letter, to the telephone, voice mail, and the fax machine, each communication advance made it easier to spread information. E-mail, though, is a quantum leap in information access.

Thanks to e-mail, information now flows freely through all levels of the business enterprise. E-mail is immediate. It's fast and it's easy. People tend to express themselves less thoughtfully in an e-mail than in a letter that needs to be signed, sealed, and delivered. Yet, the written word, no matter how hastily it's delivered, still has power. It demands we take it seriously.

What you put in writing today can literally travel around the world in minutes. It can be forwarded on to other parties, which can create problems.

In one company I worked for, a sales representative sent an e-mail to the entire company all but announcing the signing of a new and important contract. She was enthusiastic. She was sharing her excitement. And I suppose she wanted to call some attention to herself. She did. One of the executives, in his own excitement forwarded the message to the chairman of the board. The chairman got so excited he wanted us to prepare a press release. At this point our sales representative got nervous and felt it necessary to send another message. "Hey," she said, "We don't actually have a deal yet." But the damage was done. I had to spend several days lowering everyone's expectations. It could have been worse. Suppose one of the recipients of her e-mail had a friend who worked for one of our competitors?

Given recent technological advances, the ability to communicate effectively has never been more important. As a sales professional, you can't afford to ignore the implications of these changes. Too often, e-mail is replacing other means of communication. As tools become more advanced, communication becomes less personal. You know less about your customers. In fact, e-mail makes it harder to get to know them because it is increasingly substituted for live contact. Have you ever exchanged e-mails with the person in the office next to you? Sometimes it takes multiple messages to resolve an issue that could have been dispensed with in one brief face-to-face conversation. In sales, whenever you send an e-mail rather than call or meet with your clients in person, you forgo an opportunity to learn more about them.

On the plus side, e-mail can speed up the sales process if used correctly. Note that I am not suggesting using e-mail in place of other communication vehicles. E-mail is one of many communication tools. It should not be used as a replacement for other forms of communication. Circumstances should dictate when an e-mail will suffice instead of a phone call or face-to-face meeting. As with any form of communication, exercising good judgment is critical. Let's look at some e-mail do's and don'ts in sales.

E-mail Do's

- Do use e-mail to schedule or confirm meetings with clients
- Do send requested information. When the customer asks for more information about your company, you can provide brochures, annual reports, and facts and figures instantly.
- Do send thank-you notes. A handwritten note is still a better choice, but there are numerous services available on the Web that offer creative, time-saving alternatives.
- Do send e-mail responses to questions raised but left unanswered at your last meeting

E-mail Don'ts

- Don't use e-mail to detail your product or service
- Don't send bad news. You may not be communicating as clearly as you think you are. There's a good chance that your message will be misinterpreted.
- Don't send sensitive information. Once you send it, there is no way to control where it goes. It can end up in your competitor's hands or in the hands of another client who may be unhappy when, for example, they become privy to a price break they didn't get. Remember that once your message is sent, it's very hard if not impossible to delete. The record is permanent. Electronic messages helped Kenneth Starr corroborate Monica Lewinsky's grand jury testimony, and the Justice Department's antitrust case against Microsoft included e-mails written by Bill Gates that seem to support the federal government's case.

E-mail Etiquette

The following tips will ensure that your e-mail etiquette is top-notch:

- Watch what you say about people and companies, including your own. Be aware that lawyers and legislators are looking for ways to redefine slander, libel, and defamation laws, questioning whether the Internet changes the current standards.

- Don't spam your customers and prospects. Unsolicited e-mail marketing messages are an unwelcome intrusion. They clog inboxes and irritate the people you are trying to reach. If you do it often enough, eventually your messages will be blocked from reaching your target.
- Get and use a spell check application. E-mail tends to be informal. We use shortcuts such as IMO (*in my* opinion) and gestures like a smiley face; we send jokes, which are fun but not always appropriate. It also pays to remember that people notice misspellings, poor or nonexistent sentence structure, and poor taste. Are you making the impression you want to make?
- Keep your messages short and to the point. According to the Direct Marketing Association, about 500 words per e-mail is the limit.
- If you include attachments, explain what they are and why you're sending them.
- End every e-mail with your name, title, company, phone, and fax numbers.
- Don't copy anyone who really doesn't have a need to know. If you are copying the big boss just to make an impression, bear in mind that the impression you make depends on a lot more than what is in your message. The executive's mood, beliefs about the topic, and any number of other things will influence the impression you make.

▶*E-mail is a supplement not a replacement*
for staying in touch.

The World Wide Web

The Internet is perhaps the single best time saver ever to come along for the sales profession. With the help of the Web, there is no excuse for not being well prepared for a sales call. Every day more businesses and associations launch Web sites. Many are loaded with information about their strategies, their triumphs, and even their foibles. You can get information about your prospect's management team and their products and services, and even download the most recent annual report of publicly traded companies.

Companies that have not seen fit to produce a Web site can still be researched by using one of the many well-known search engines to find information about them. Web sites such as *www.Hoovers.com* and *www.Individual.com* offer comprehensive information about companies in every industry segment. You can even get mailing lists targeted for your markets at sites such as *USAData.com*. If your prospect has been in the news, chances are excellent that you can find out why.

Obviously the same can be said about your own company. Check out your own company's site on a regular basis. It's hard to look good if your customer knows something about you that you don't know. Naturally, the Web is a great place to learn more about your competition as well. In the same way that reading your competitor's magazine ads is informative, their Web site will tell you how your competition is selling to your customers.

Numerous new business uses for the World Wide Web appear almost daily. For example, there are e-commerce companies offering technology that permits you to do product demonstrations from your office while your customers observe from their own offices on their PCs. Although the new technology is exciting, be sure to ask yourself if the latest wizardry is an improvement over alternative means of communication. While a live Web-based demo might save you a trip and airfare, it may not be an adequate—not to mention good—substitute for a face-to-face meeting. Don't let fancy technology cloud your judgment.

▶ *The Web is an indispensable communication sales tool.*
Get comfortable with it.

Chapter 9

A Short Course on Public Speaking

A Communication Skill You Must Have

As a sales professional, most of your sales calls take place in one-on-one or small group situations. Yet, as your career advances, you will find it necessary to address large groups. When you're selling big-ticket items, for example, it's likely you will be asked to make presentations in front of demanding, high-level decision-makers. This differs from one-on-one conversations in several ways. For one thing, you will be reciting a monologue of sorts—not unlike a performer. Next, you will be standing rather than sitting. Although this may seem a minor difference, standing puts you in a leadership role, raising listeners' expectations.

Speaking in front of groups does not come naturally to everyone. If you have the desire to sell at the highest levels and move up the corporate ladder, you must learn the basics of public speaking. Effective presentation skills can help you reach the top levels of your industry. If public speaking is a chore for you, take heart. With practice, you can learn to be a dynamic speaker.

There are numerous books that provide instruction on public speaking. Reading one of these books would be a great way to get basic information about the topic. Ron Hoff's book *I Can See You Naked* is a classic. However, nothing beats getting out there and doing it over and over until you learn the craft.

This chapter will familiarize you with the basics of public speaking. Each section focuses on one of the three distinct aspects of a presentation: preparation, practice, and performance.

▶*Every organization has a place for skilled presenters.*

Preparation

Public speaking is different from a conversation. As the speaker, you are the center of attention and a leader with responsibilities to your audience. As in most sales situations, your primary objective is to inform or perhaps to persuade your listeners. Here are the seven basic steps to help prepare for a presentation or speech.

1. Make Sure You Understand the Assignment

If you're asked to make a speech, there are several questions you should ask before committing. It will save you a lot of trouble and worry later. I learned my lesson when the head nurse at a state psychiatric hospital facility asked me to say a few words to some of the doctors on the medical staff. She said it would be informal, and I pictured a small conference room where I would chat with four or five doctors.

When I arrived for the meeting she took me down to the auditorium, where at least fifty doctors were assembled. Moreover, I was a participant on a panel that included the head of the state medicaid office. I was petrified. I managed to get through it somehow, but I have never assumed anything about a presentation since.

There are several commonsense questions you should ask before committing to a speech:

- How many will be in attendance?
- What time of day will I be speaking?
- Will there be other presenters?
- How long do they expect me to speak?
- Where will the meeting take place?
- Can the room accommodate audiovisual equipment?

2. Examine Your Topic

Look beyond what you want to say and consider what you should say. Deciding what to say depends on your objectives, your audience, and their expectations. Often, you have to balance what you would like to say with the audience's expectations. Make sure you are up-to-date on all aspects of your topic. There's nothing worse than ignoring a growing trend or controversy. If you ignore their needs, you won't really be heard.

3. Analyze Your Audience

As soon as you agree to make a speech, start asking questions about your audience. Consider demographics like gender and age range: Who has spoken to this group lately? Are they decision-makers? Are you addressing members of an association or an executive management team? The answers to these questions will help you decide on the most effective way to deliver your message. If you're using audiovisuals, your selection of media and color may be different for a crowd in their twenties than for one in their sixties. You will also have a good idea of the type of comments and observations to include. For example, if you were meeting with a group of middle-aged female executives, references to baseball players who played during the Sixties would probably be meaningless for most of them.

4. Do Your Homework

Even if you know your topic well, it can't hurt to do a little research. Find some statistics, quotes, or anecdotes that will support your facts and opinions. It will add credibility to your presentation. Your talk will be more entertaining and you will feel more confident knowing you are well prepared.

5. Write It Down

Write your speech down as you plan to say it. If you are more comfortable with an outline, by all means do that instead. Once you see your words in writing, you'll be able to edit the speech for weaknesses. The writing process is also an opportunity to organize your thoughts. As discussed earlier, every presentation has an opening, a body, and a close. Each part serves a distinct purpose. A speech is no different. Writing your speech will also help you become more comfortable with your material and increase your confidence.

6. Get Ready for the Q&A Session

When preparing for the Q&A, put yourself in the audience's shoes for a moment. What questions will they ask? Write them down and think about whether you could eliminate some of the questions by including more information in your speech. If so, you may want to address these questions in your presentation. Likewise, don't feel that you have to cover every possible angle in the speech. Remember that your time will be limited. And, similar to a traditional sales call, the question-and-answer segment of your talk is an opportunity to engage your audience in conversation.

7. Check Out the Room

If possible, get to the meeting before the attendees arrive so you can familiarize yourself with your surroundings. Take your assigned seat and practice walking up to the lectern or the position you will take when you give your talk. Look out at the room, taking time to notice details. Acclimating yourself to the environment will relax you when it's actually time to speak. If you can't arrange to get the room to yourself, get there as early as possible anyway. Spend some time chatting with your host and the attendees. Simply being in the room will allow you to warm up.

"When you're prepared, you're more confident.
When you have a strategy, you're more comfortable."
—Fred Couples

Practice

Your father said it. Your teachers and coaches said it, too. Practice makes perfect. Although perfection is hard to achieve, practice offers obvious benefits. Practicing your presentation will definitely improve your performance.

You should practice your speech at least three times from start to finish. You must practice aloud to get a full return on your investment. It isn't necessary to do it in front of friends or family members. The mirror is fine. Better yet, tape yourself and play it back. Practicing out loud helps you get comfortable with the words and sounds, giving you more confidence in your ability to deliver the speech in front of an audience.

Speaking your written words out loud may also surprise you. You'll notice that some words that work well on paper don't have the intended effect when spoken aloud. Rehearsal gives you one more opportunity to refine your presentation. Assuming you aren't reading from a script, each time you deliver your presentation, you will find yourself altering your choice of words.

As you rehearse your words, you will begin to feel familiar with them and your confidence will rise. Don't try to memorize your speech. Just get comfortable with the words. Think about how you can use body language to add impact to your presentation. Let your body do what it would do if you were having a conversation on your topic with a colleague. Finally, remember that a well-placed pause can add as much punch as the actual words you say.

Be sure to time yourself. How long is your speech? If you are running twenty-eight minutes long and your allotted time is thirty minutes, you will want to do some editing. For one thing, your actual time may well be longer when you give your talk "live." You also want to leave enough time to take questions. If you're running longer than you expected, go back over each part of your speech and cut anything that you don't really need.

"Skill comes from practice."
—Chinese proverb

Performance

If you've done your homework and practiced your presentation, a winning performance is practically assured. Now it's time for you to put it all together. Your performance begins as soon as you enter the building. Your demeanor will make an immediate impression on everyone. Exude confidence, even if you feel nervous or unsure. Remember, there is a difference between being confident and being cocky. People can easily see when someone is behaving arrogantly. Avoid such behaviors so you don't turn off your audience before your talk. Remember, quiet confidence and a genuine smile work best in this situation.

Five Keys to a Winning Performance
Overcome Stage Fright

If you're well prepared, the only thing that can interfere with a good performance is nervousness or stage fright. Although some people don't experience any performance anxiety, it's natural to feel some nervousness when you make a presentation. In fact, nervous energy is a good thing. Harness that energy to enhance your performance. If you feel overwhelmed by anxiety, there are a variety of ways you can relieve your stress. For example, deep breathing often has a calming effect. If you stop to think about why you feel so nervous, you will discover that it usually stems from being overly concerned with how you will be perceived by the audience. If you focus on delivering your message as well as you can with a sincere desire to be helpful to your listeners, your stage fright will recede and even disappear.

Make Eye Contact

Making eye contact is an effective way to make sure your audience is listening and that they understand your message. As you deliver your speech, make eye contact with the people in the room. Try to concentrate on one person until your eyes meet momentarily. Then, move on to the next person and so on. When you look people in the eye, it shows you are confident and comfortable with your topic.

Use Body Language

Use natural gestures and facial expressions to emphasize key points. If you use humor, smile to let the audience know it's okay to laugh. Don't be afraid to be a bit more animated than you would be in casual conversation. In a large group setting, more expansive gestures are effective.

Give Them Some Vocal Variety

Vocal variety helps hold your listeners' interest. Don't be afraid to use your voice to impact your words. Raising your voice, lowering it, picking up the pace, and slowing down are all time-tested rhetorical devices at your disposal. Remember that pauses help listeners absorb your message.

Don't Read

Reading your speech is deadly. People tend to read in a monotone voice, picking up speed as the speech progresses. Reading lacks spontaneity so there's little if any opportunity to connect with your audience. Unless you are a very skilled reader, it's best to work from notes. While some experts advise speaking without notes, less experienced speakers are better off having notes to refer to because it helps them avoid leaving out any relevant information. This is a disservice to your audience. You don't have to refer to your notes, but if they are right in front of you, you don't have to worry about losing your train of thought either.

▶*Your performance will mirror the intensity of your preparation and practice.*

Chapter 10

Advanced Sales Communication

Words Matter

It's important to be conscious of the impact our choice of words or a turn of phrase can have. Whether it's the first impression you make or the reaction you get to your proposal, good or bad, it might well be derived from a single word. Substituting another word might alter the result. Unfortunately, there is no sure-fire formula that guarantees you will always find the right word. In fact, words can either delight or offend, depending on the circumstances. For example, while four-letter words are usually devastating, they may be strangely fitting under just the right circumstances.

A few years ago the CEO of a company introduced his presentation to prospective investors by saying, "We have this *canned* presentation for you today." Most of us like to feel special. When we are asking people to do business with us, it makes sense to treat them that way. The word *canned* says, "I didn't go to any special trouble for you. I certainly did not consider whether I should address any unique needs you may have. I will probably give the exact presentation to another group this afternoon."

One word, several negative messages. While I'm certain the CEO didn't intend to offend his audience, his word choice was unfortunate.

A poor choice of words can cost you a sale you should have made with no trouble. When I worked for a technology firm, a sales representative who was calling on us for the first time asked me, "Isn't your company going bankrupt?" I respected his right to ask this type of question on behalf of his firm. Since we were a publicly traded company, our status was obvious. We were struggling to meet earnings projections but paying our bills. Asking the question so directly forced me into a defensive posture.

He should have said something like this: "I saw your fourth quarter earnings report recently. Our CFO has some concerns. What is the outlook from your perspective?" By avoiding an inflammatory word such as *bankruptcy,* it would have allowed me to respond without putting me on the spot.

Remember, too, that our words have a way of painting pictures in the customer's mind. Not long ago, a representative of a software firm called on me to demonstrate his firm's new product. He told me that his company had recently decided to use the product in its business. He said it this way: "We're learning to eat our own dog food." That just didn't work for me. Use words that create an attractive image in the customer's mind.

As we discussed earlier, developing your vocabulary gives you more choices when communicating an idea, highlighting the benefits of your service, asking an important question, or responding to a touchy situation. Choosing your words carefully is as much a matter of being thoughtful as it is of being articulate. Find and use the best words to make your meaning clear.

I firmly believe that people who consciously consider word choice are less likely to make mistakes. With a positive attitude and conscious effort, you will find the best words to suit most circumstances.

Here's one more example of how much words matter. I was the chief operating officer of a health care company specializing in disease management. Wanting to build teamwork and morale,

I was sending the entire company e-mails every day with inspirational quotes. I thought a quote from Stephen Jobs was a particularly creative way of pointing out how much good we could do by helping people with chronic illness. So I sent it.

Jobs was quoted in the book, *In the Company of Giants* (Rama Jager and Raphael Ortiz [New York: McGraw Hill, 1997]): " . . . in the end it's the work that binds. That's why it's so important to pick very important things to do because it's very hard to get people motivated to make a breakfast cereal. It takes something that's worth doing."

The next day I got an e-mail back from one of the nurses. "My husband works for Quaker Oats," she said, "Around our house, we think that's pretty important too."

> *"Man does not live by words alone, despite*
> *the fact that sometimes he has to eat them."*
> —Adlai Stevenson

How Many People Are You Meeting With?

The number of people participating in a conversation affects communication. When scheduling a meeting with a customer, it's important to know how many people will be in attendance and what role they play in the organization. The basic rule of thumb is that intimacy declines as more people are involved in a discussion. As the number of people increases, we become more formal and less familiar in our speech. As a sales professional, you should be consciously aware of the impact the number of people in a sales situation can have on the outcome of your meeting. When planning your meeting, be sure to take this into consideration.

One-on-One Meetings

In most instances, the most favorable situation is a one-on-one meeting with your client.

One-on-one situations are the best time to really get to know your customer. People have a natural tendency to let their guard down a bit when they know there is no one else around to monitor (or perhaps judge) their behavior. As trust builds between you and your client, your relationship may permit a certain familiarity. This is a valuable privilege, but be cautious. While you may have achieved a certain level of intimacy with your customer in one-on-one meetings, be extremely cautious about displaying the same familiarity in front of others. It can be a source of embarrassment to your customer and you. Play it safe when others are present by keeping your words and tone strictly professional.

One-on-one meetings are also the best way to resolve disagreements. A lot of potential problems can be avoided by simply talking face-to-face, without others in the room. For example, take the situation in which the customer has told his colleagues in advance that he has certain non-negotiable demands. If those colleagues attend the meeting, it can be extremely difficult to make progress in the "non-negotiable" areas because the tough bargainer feels he can't afford to lose face with his colleagues. Your chances of reaching an agreement under those conditions are significantly reduced. When it's just the two of you, both parties are more likely to be flexible.

Small Groups

Problem-solving is an activity that lends itself best to small groups of three or four participants, allowing the benefit of different perspectives in a manageable environment. The more people involved, the harder it is to assess and solve a problem. If you are confronted with a situation in which a problem-solving group is too large, take your primary contact aside and suggest scheduling another session with a smaller group as soon as possible.

Large Groups

If you are meeting with a larger group, your presentation becomes more formal. It's important to plan ahead to ensure a high level of participation in this situation. If you want to encourage feedback, keep in mind that the larger the group, the lower the participation level. Many people are uncomfortable speaking up in front of "an audience." You must be prepared to act as a facilitator. A skilled facilitator involves everyone in the discussion, demonstrating respect for ideas as well as contrary opinions. In the facilitator's role, you have an opportunity to guide the discussion. You can make your point and still bring the group to consensus, ensuring that everyone shares a successful outcome.

In larger groups you are also forced to deal with the reality that different people hearing the same words can come away with substantially different interpretations of what's been said and may come to opposite conclusions based on what they've heard. On critical points, you must seek out these differences. Ask questions to ensure understanding. Rephrase your key points to elicit comments. Remember, the more people there are in the room, the greater the chance for misunderstandings. By all means, when the crowd is large, keep it simple.

Quite often, especially when it's a big-ticket item at stake, the sales process requires the customer to provide additional information at a later date. The more participants in the meeting, the harder it is to keep track of who has agreed to do what. Take notes and make it a point to follow up afterward to confirm your understanding of what each person has promised to do. As one sales professional said, "The more people who are involved, the more likely I'm going to deal with a pocket veto— people promising to do things and not doing them." Don't let that happen to you. Follow up.

We also make adjustments depending on who is involved in the conversation. In everyday life, for example, the way you converse with your spouse when you are alone is different from the way you interact with each other when your children are present. If you're socializing with another couple, the dynamics are again different, and you adjust the communication accordingly.

Likewise, in a sales situation, communication dynamics often change when an executive joins the group. When it's the CEO, the change is often pronounced. Members of the CEO's staff will likely look for signs from the CEO for approval or disapproval and act accordingly. Usually, the CEO will do most of the talking. Take note of who appears to interact most freely with the top executive. Chances are good that these people are key influencers. Don't ignore them. Seek them out; encourage their opinions. Sometimes you can gauge the prospect's interest level by who attends the meeting. Certainly having executives present is usually a sign of interest. These people are waiting to be sold. React properly and reap the rewards.

▶*Adapt your communication strategy*
to the size of your audience.

How to Make an Introduction

Too often, sales professionals treat introductions as an afterthought. They handle them like a common pleasantry, no different than saying *gesundheit* after someone sneezes. Yet, introductions are a great opportunity to set the tone and the agenda for the meeting.

When you are required to introduce someone in a sales situation, assess what the purpose of the meeting is beforehand. If it is merely a "getting to know you" session, your introduction might be different than if you have brought your senior management in to help you negotiate an agreement.

Consider this scenario as a "don't" when making introductions: A sales representative is calling on an important customer and his boss is going along. Naturally, the representative is a bit apprehensive about making introductions. When it comes time to introduce the boss, the sales rep, out of nervousness, blows it with a bad joke. "This is Mary Green. She's my boss, so be nice to me today." While the joke may get a polite chuckle from the customer, the meeting begins with an uncomfortable moment.

If your boss simply wants to get to know your customer, your initial introduction should state that fact and explain why it is important to your client: "Meet Karen Jackson, our vice president of sales. Karen wanted to meet you, Bob, because we want you to be comfortable calling her if I can't be reached. Karen's been with our company for five years. If I'm not available, she can help you resolve any issue that might arise."

Your introduction should also include an icebreaker, mentioning interests that Karen and Bob share or similar backgrounds, such as being from the same city. A good introduction minimizes the risk of awkward silences.

If the meeting is of a more serious nature, your introduction should acknowledge the situation by again making clear the reason you have brought someone with you. In this situation, your introduction should focus more on the credentials of your partner.

Gina, I've asked Tim Peters to join me today. He's here to help us get a handle on the concerns you expressed about integrating our software with your current information system.

As our director of information technology, Tim frequently works with customers to resolve similar issues. He also has ten years of experience with the BigBox database applications you are running today. By the way, Gina, like you, Tim is a mountain bike enthusiast.

Notice that the introduction establishes Tim's credentials and introduces a subject establishing common ground between Tim and Gina.

Be sure not to overdo introductions. Saying, "Tim is the most knowledgeable person in the entire industry, and he has very exciting ideas that I know you will love," only sets up Tim for failure. Perhaps you are just trying to be generous with your coworker, but what you have really done is made his job more difficult.

A good introduction will help you keep everyone focused on the agenda. When you do your pre-call planning, include a strategy for introductions.

> ▶*Don't be casual about introductions.*
> *Make them work for you.*

The Art of Storytelling

For centuries, storytelling has brought groups of people together on common ground. People love stories. Don't be afraid to use stories to enhance your presentation. Stories are a magnificent way to illustrate a point while helping your customer remember it. Stories, like other forms of communication, not only appeal to our intellect but also touch our hearts.

The stories you tell should be true. They should be entertaining while making a point that advances your cause. Shorter stories are usually better. The longer the story is, the higher the payoff has to be to satisfy those who invested their time listening to you.

Health care happens to be a field that abounds with story material. Inspirational stories or tales that bring tears to listener's eyes are plentiful. Helping sick people overcome adversity and achieve a measure of happiness or relief is something we all identify with.

When I was trying to sell physicians on the idea of providing specialized breathing equipment in the home for patients with serious lung disease, I could have said something like this, "Doctor, clinical studies demonstrate that ventilator therapy improves a patient's quality of life, permitting him to take part in activities of daily living."

Although the statement is accurate, it certainly doesn't paint any pictures in the doctor's mind. What if I had a real-life story instead? Suppose I said, "Doctor, three months ago, Doctor Clark in Titusville put a seventy-six-year-old patient on our ventilation therapy program at home. This man was spending his entire day in a rocking chair because he needed all of his energy just to breathe. Now he goes trout fishing three times a week."

A story personalizes your product or service. In this case, the story appeals to the doctor's ultimate reason for practicing medicine: helping people. In addition, the story references a professional colleague endorsing the concept.

When using storytelling in your presentations, think like a reporter writing a human-interest piece. Ask lots of probing questions. Get as much detail as you can. The man doesn't just go fishing. He fishes for trout. The more details you provide, the better your story is.

Your coworkers, especially the customer service staff, can supply you with wonderful success stories. Your customers are another source of golden nuggets. Ask them. Keep your eyes and ears wide open every day. Once you start looking for good stories, I promise you'll have no trouble finding them.

Stories are easy to collect, but don't rely exclusively on your memory to retain them. Start and keep a story log. It will come in handy when you need a story to help you make a point. The good news is that stories are quite adaptable. Very often you can make an existing story suit your purpose rather than trying to find a new story to match your point. Searching through your story log for a story that might work is a lot easier than trying to remember something that might match your needs.

> *"An honest tale speeds best being plainly told."*
> —Shakespeare, *Richard III*

Staying in Touch

You need a communication strategy after you make the sale. It's easy to be attentive when a sale is at stake or you just closed a big deal. But are you reaching out and communicating after you make the sale? It can be tempting to move on to new horizons once you make the sale, but it's risky. Ignoring your customer sends a powerful message. It says, "I don't need you anymore." In most cases though, you will need the customer again and again. It's a fact that current customers are easier to sell to than new ones, especially if you maintain good relationships.

Staying in touch with clients pays big dividends. Done properly it cements the relationship, creating a bond that isn't easily broken. If you are loyal to your clients, they will buy from you again and again, even if they change jobs. They'll buy from you even if you go to work for your competitor.

Staying in touch with your client is an art that requires some imagination and organizational skills. Fortunately, there are a number of tools available today. Contact management databases such as Goldmine and ACT are excellent tools you can buy to support your efforts. Programs like these help you to keep track of important dates and events as well as actions you've taken or plan to take. You can also record personal information about your clients like birthdays and anniversaries.

There are many ways to stay in touch. Here are a few ideas that should help get your own creative juices flowing.

Regular Status Reports

After you've made the sale, make a special effort to update your customer on the status of your business relationship.

In some cases, that might mean reports showing ongoing purchases. In others, it might mean demonstrating product or service performance. For example, if you provide a billing and collection service, you can supply regular reports on how much is collected. You can also inquire about your client's satisfaction with your service. By frequently communicating your interest in your customer's situation, you will build a stellar relationship. Your chances of additional sales will improve dramatically. You will also reduce the likelihood of unpleasant surprises. Many customers simply won't tell you they are unhappy unless you ask them for feedback.

News Clippings

When you come across industry-related news items that might be of interest to one of your clients, clip the item and send it along with a note. Your note can be as simple as "I thought you might find this interesting."

If there is a particular point you want to make that is relevant to the article, add that as well. For example, "Looks like energy prices are going up again, a problem for both of us. Let's discuss it in our meeting next week."

Don't waste your customer's time with frivolous items or major events they are surely aware of. There is plenty of useful information out there. Thanks to e-mail, it's a simple matter to forward an interesting news item along with your personal note.

One woman I know searches the newspapers and trade journals for announcements of promotions or awards earned by her customers. She cuts them out, has them laminated, and sends them to the recipient with a congratulatory note. It's a thoughtful gesture.

Greeting Cards

Sending greeting cards is an effective means to communicate with your customer. Birthday cards or cards acknowledging a promotion or the recent death of a loved one are especially appreciated and memorable. Of course, many people send Christmas or Season's Greetings cards. But not many people send Halloween or Thanksgiving cards. If your customer is say, Irish, send her a St. Patrick's Day card. Your thoughtfulness will be remembered especially because it wasn't expected. A greeting card with a handwritten note tells customers you are thinking about them.

Phone Calls

I have a few suppliers who call periodically just to say they are keeping in touch. They ask if everything is going well. I usually say things are fine and that ends the call. I don't mind hearing from them but after a while, I can't help but wonder what they are trying to achieve. It feels as though I'm having my pulse taken, after which I'm pronounced fine, at least in their minds. This type of call doesn't add value to the relationship. It certainly doesn't grow the relationship. I hate to admit it, but in some small way it diminishes my respect for the caller.

When you decide to keep in touch via the phone, you must communicate something beyond your desire for your customer's continued well-being. Have some news to share, whether it's a new product soon to be released or an update of recent purchases. Don't be subtle about this. Point out why you are sharing the information. Usually, a legitimate business pretext for the call gives you permission to socialize for a few minutes without appearing needy or worse, insensitive to your client's time.

▶*Don't be a stranger to your customers.*
Your competition is knocking on their doors.

A Few Phrases You Can Eliminate from Your Repertoire

We all have pet phrases that we fall back on when we are in conversation. We use these phrases to jump-start a conversation or to respond to a question. As a sales professional, you can't afford the luxury of using words and phrases that might diminish your chances of success. Here are a few common examples:

I know you've heard this before, *but* . . . . Recently I met with an executive representing an Internet-based purchasing service who said, "You probably have heard this five times before, but . . . " He insisted on telling us the story anyway. Although it was surely unintentional, his message was, "I don't value your time."

Yes, but . . . . Pretending to agree and then taking it back is a frequently used device. It doesn't work. People know you've dismissed their argument as soon as they hear the word *but*.

To be perfectly honest with you . . . . When you make this statement, you risk giving people the impression that you may not have been honest in the past. This phrase is often used as a rhetorical device not unlike "by the way" or "I'm not sure if I mentioned this but." To be safe, avoid phrases such as *to be honest, let me be frank,* and *candidly*.

To make a long story short . . . . By the time you say this, you've probably gone on too long already. If it is a long story, tell it. Remember, the longer the story, the bigger the payoff.

Other fillers . . . . Avoid qualifying your statements with phrases and words such as *sort of, kind of, like, you know, I was wondering if.* These choices weaken whatever point you are trying to make. Typically, these terms are used to soften something that might concern or annoy a customer. However, using them makes you appear weak, unprepared, and unsure.

> ▶*Fillers always weaken your message.*
> *Eliminate them from your vocabulary.*

Are You Speaking the Same Language?

When managed care was a hot topic in health care, I was hired by a large home care company to sell its services to managed care organizations. These companies—HMOs, PPOs, Blue Cross, and Blue Shield Plans—all spoke the same language, meaning they had similar problems and similar interests.

One reason for my success in selling to managed care organizations was that I spent many years working for Blue Cross as a buyer of services. I knew the lingo. I used to be the guy who sat on the other side of the table, listening to health care providers make sales presentations. Since I knew what the managed care hot buttons were, I was able to tell my story in terms that appealed to their needs.

I have also taught salespeople about managed care and how to sell their products to these organizations. In the process I learned an interesting thing about language. Just because I explained the inner workings of managed care organizations, how they operate, their priorities, fears, and prerogatives didn't mean the sales force grasped it. No matter how basic I tried to make it, too often salespeople left our meeting with that deer-in-the-headlights look.

Quite by accident, I figured out why. I was returning from lunch with my boss one day when he decided to stop at a liquor store to buy a bottle of wine for a dinner party he was having. He used terms like *varietals* to describe the grapes of a particular wine and *tannins* to describe acidity levels in red wines and so on. I had no idea what he was talking about.

I discovered that until I learned the language of wine I could not really absorb the details, not to mention appreciate the nuances associated with the winemaking process and ultimately wine tasting.

Your company and your industry have languages of their own. In fact, every business and industry develops language that applies specifically to its specialty. One of the most prolific is the computer and software industry; consider CPUs, ERP, frame relay, XML, and so on. Health care is another example. The field is loaded with initials and acronyms to describe patient status and location: ER, OR, ICU, NPO, TID.

Jargon is a word that describes an industry's unique language. It serves a very useful purpose beyond shorthand. Jargon provides a way to signal others in the group that you a knowledgeable insider. You are part of the tribe. These terms become part of our everyday vocabulary because they also serve a practical purpose. Acronyms, handy shorthand for longer terms, serve a similar purpose.

It's easy to forget that not everyone knows what these terms mean. We become so used to using them around the office that it's easy, even natural, to toss these words around when calling on a customer. Many people simply will not tell you they don't know the meaning of a word or term. They don't want to appear uninformed, so they smile, nod, and let it pass. However, that doesn't mean they aren't struggling. They are wondering if they missed something important that could come back to bite them later.

If your customer isn't familiar with your industry's special language, you are swimming against the current in muddy water. Keep that in mind when you are selling a product or service, especially if it's a new concept. Don't expect to sell your services the first time out. Develop a communication plan that gives your prospect enough time to grasp your language. Use nontechnical language. If you must use a technical or industry-specific term, look for signs of confusion and ask immediately if your customer needs further clarification.

▶*Make sure you and your customers speak the same language. They'll appreciate it.*

Handling Mistakes

Mistakes happen in business. There's no avoiding them. Shipments are sometimes wrong or late. Products arrive damaged. Services are subject to human error. I like to see mistakes as a wonderful opportunity.

The way you handle mistakes tells your customer far more about you and your company than just about any other situation you will encounter. Remember that when you make a mistake, whether shipping the wrong item or failing to deliver a promised service, you may well be putting your client in a bad light with a supervisor. When your company makes a significant error, your clients want and need your support more than ever.

If you can make a prompt and thorough recovery, you can put your relationship on better footing than it was before the incident occurred. To do this, you'll need an effective communication strategy to deal with problems. Here are some basic rules you can follow to help you say and do the right thing.

- *Start with a short but firm apology.* Don't make excuses. Don't blame your company. Simply say, "I am sorry this happened. It shouldn't have happened and I take full responsibility. I'll do my best to make sure it doesn't happen again."
- *Never be defensive.* Even if you are right, it won't help to accuse the customer of incorrectly filling out an order form. Solve the problem and then spend some time re-educating your client on how to follow proper procedure.

- *Don't minimize the problem.* For example, if there is a crisis in your warehouse or your company just switched to a new computer system, explain the situation and let your customer know when it will be fixed. If it is going to be a while before things are back to normal, ask them to bear with you. Minimizing the problem is the worst thing you can do. If the situation gets worse, your credibility will shrink with every new delay. If you're honest with your customers, they will support you.
- *Explain what you will do to resolve the problem.* Whether you give them a discount, replace the item free of charge, or perform the service again, tell them exactly what you will do and when it will be done.
- *Follow up.* Keep your customers apprised of the situation. Once you have resolved the problem, be sure they are satisfied with the results.

Handling mistakes properly gives you the opportunity to strengthen the foundation of your relationship. A casual or inappropriate response can weaken the foundation you worked so carefully to build. While customers know that you cannot personally control every aspect of your business, they expect you, as their designated representative, to resolve the problem.

▶*Mistakes are opportunities. Make the most of them.*

When the Customer Says No

You've worked hard to get the business. You played fair. The customer has been making buying signs for weeks. Then you get the dreaded phone call. Your client has decided to go with your competitor this time. You've lost the business. It's normal to feel angry, disappointed, frustrated, or betrayed. Yet, as a sales professional, you know that sometimes you will lose.

In spite of your best efforts, you won't always get the order.

How do you respond? You could say what one HMO executive told a hospital CEO upon learning that the hospital would buy its health care coverage elsewhere. "You'll regret this. In six months you'll be back on your knees asking for the same deal. But it won't be there." While anger in such moments can overwhelm common sense, it pays to keep a cool head, and it is certainly appropriate to express your disappointment.

> *I am very disappointed to hear this news. I would appreciate it if you could take a few minutes to review your decision with me. It would be very helpful to know who you selected, what the deciding factors were, and whether I could have done something different that might have changed the outcome.*

There is a small chance that the customer will say something that points to a misunderstanding about your offer. Perhaps they will express a tiny doubt that might create a new opening that could revive the deal. However, assuming the decision is final, once the customer has answered your questions, it's important to thank them for giving you an opportunity to bid on the business. Let the client know that you intend to stay in touch and that you will be happy to provide assistance in the future.

A few things you should avoid when the customer says no:

- *Don't make it personal.* For example, hinting that you might lose your job over this, suggesting that the process was flawed, or accusing the customer of dealing in bad faith won't change the outcome. It will only reinforce doubts the customer may have had.
- *Don't try to plant seeds of doubt about the wisdom of their choice.* It's insulting to the customer. However, if you are aware of a legitimate and important issue about the firm that won the business, make sure you stay in touch with your

customer frequently. If the storm breaks, you'll be there with a bucket to bale them out.

- *Assuming you will still be calling on the customer occasionally, don't remind them of your disappointment when you see them.*

Finally, remember that "no" is never final. Things change. You'll have another opportunity to sell something to customers who say no for now. By keeping your disappointment in proper perspective, you can develop a communication strategy that positions you for the future.

▶*Start working on your next sale
the minute your customer says no.*

When You Must Say No

In Mario Puzo's bestselling novel, *The Godfather*, there is a scene with Michael Corleone in which his father, the godfather, explains how to say no to someone. He says, "You have to take time with people. You can't say no very often, and then you have to make it sound like a yes." The point, of course, is that you must exercise patience when you must say no.

It isn't easy to say no when the customer asks for something. To begin with, salespeople tend to be pleasers. Oftentimes, salespeople are afraid that if they disappoint their customer, that customer will buy from someone else.

Customers can be unreasonably demanding in some cases. They want more free samples, a bigger price concession, tickets to the World Series. While it's delightful to say yes, saying no also serves a useful purpose. Saying no to a customer's request is a great way to test the status of your relationship. Are you really valued as a resource or just a commodity?

Customers who value you as a resource are far more likely

to respect your decision than those who are merely interested in gaining a short-term advantage. Of course, saying no gracefully can make an enormous difference. Here are some quick do's and don'ts when you have to break bad news.

Do's
- Prepare a thorough explanation before delivering bad news to your customer
- Be brief, direct, and firm when saying no to your customer
- Use an empathetic tone
- Suggest reasonable alternatives

Don'ts
- Don't blame the customer
- Don't blame your company
- Don't let the customer's reaction throw you

If you've been honest, they get over it. Avoid the urge to apologize for saying no. Certainly it's fine to say, "I'm sorry, but I can't do that right now." Don't apologize profusely, however, for something that doesn't make sense for your company. Doing so can risk your credibility.

You may also be tempted to make vague promises about making it up to your customer in the future. While circumstances might dictate that you make such an offer, you are only setting yourself up for trouble later. Some customers like to remind you of that promise long after you feel you repaid your debt. Remember, customers sometimes make unreasonable demands. From time to time, they ask for things that might not even be in their own best interest. Saying no can be a favor to them.

▶ *Saying no is a rarely practiced but necessary skill.*

Don't Knock the Competition

A sales representative from an oxygen equipment manufacturer paid us a call. His equipment was designed to regulate the flow of oxygen in a patient's home. He extolled the virtues of his product, explaining that it was superior to competitor brands because his product used more brass than the others. Using brass instead of aluminum, he said, greatly reduced the risk of an explosion and fire. Up to that point he was doing well. Then, he pulled out several photos showing tests his company had conducted on competitors' equipment. The quality of the photos was poor, but it was apparent that his product stood up to the test significantly better than any of the others. The photos were not labeled. There was no report by an independent party to substantiate the test results. We heard nothing about test conditions or scientific methods. Frankly, we were shocked. We listened politely, but we could not help wondering about his strategy.

Don't knock the competition is a rule most sales professionals learn early in their careers. The reason for the rule is obvious. Your products and services should stand on their own merit. Knocking the competition really says, "Their product is even worse than ours." Moreover, if the customer is already doing business with the company you're knocking, it implies that the customer isn't very astute. If you're criticizing your competitor's sales representatives, marketing strategy, and their product without proof, you're off base. Taking a cheap shot won't help you win your customer's confidence.

While knocking the competition is foolish, there is nothing wrong with talking about them. Asking questions about your competitors can be a rewarding experience. Ask what your competitors do best and how they can improve. There is nothing wrong with inquiring about areas such as warranties and on-time delivery performance. The answers will give you valuable clues. You can learn what it takes to please your customer and how to avoid losing them as well. Pointing out the differences between the competitor's product and yours is also a legitimate topic of discussion.

If you must talk about the competition:

- *Know what you are talking about.* It helps to know as much about your competition as possible. Understanding their strengths and weaknesses can help you articulate what differentiates your product or service from theirs. Company Web sites have certainly made research easier than ever. There's no excuse for being uninformed.
- *Speak kindly about competitors whenever possible.* What you say can easily get back to them. Someday, you just might want to work for them.
- *Realize that the customer will take any negative comments you make, no matter how accurate, with a grain of salt.* They are obliged to consider the source.
- *Never express a negative thought about the competition's sales representative, even if encouraged or provoked.* Remember you are both members of the same profession.

Let's look at a few specific situations involving your competitors that are likely to arise in the course of a sales call.

The customer asks your opinion of Company *A*'s hot new product. How should you respond? Acknowledge the uniqueness of the product. Encourage the customer to try it if they feel it might meet their needs. Briefly point out any significant drawbacks they may not be aware of. Then describe your organization's alternative solution.

The customer asks if you've heard about the government investigation of Company *X*. If you have heard about it, say so. Then say that you hope for the industry's sake they can clear it up quickly. Avoid expressing any opinions about the merits of the investigation or what impact it might have on Company *X*'s future.

The customer complains about Company *D*'s performance, expressing anger about poor service. Empathize with the customer but resist the temptation to pile on. Emphasize your company's service record and commitment to quality.

> ▶*Talk about the competition the way
> you hope they talk about you.*

When the Customer Steps Out of Line

Salespeople are taught early in their careers that the customer is always right. There are good reasons for this philosophy. More often than we might care to admit, the differences between our product and the competition's isn't significant. Even when there are some meaningful differences, we can still lose the sale simply because the customer likes the other guy more.

Believe me, as a customer, it takes very little time to realize that you are being deferred to. Like the CEO whose jokes are always funny, whose insights are always on target, the customer is treated like royalty. It's a heady feeling. It's tempting for customers to take liberties, saying and doing things they wouldn't even consider under different circumstances, certain that you won't retaliate.

In most situations, the best course of action is to take it in stride, swallow hard, and say nothing. Not responding to bad behavior will usually make the point without embarrassing your client. But what if the customer crosses the line? What if he insults your integrity, curses you with a string of four-letter words, makes sexual innuendos, or embarrasses you in front of your coworkers? Is there ever a situation when you should assert yourself, and let the customer have it between the eyes? The answer depends on the circumstances.

First, consider whether this behavior is surprising or part of a behavior pattern that has become progressively more abusive. If it's the former, it might be wise to let it pass or respond in a gentle manner, such as saying, "Is everything all right?" People who are normally cordial will rarely step out of character. Something may be going on in your customer's life, at work or at home, that has him on edge. Expressing genuine concern gives the customer an opportunity to reflect on his behavior. He may even tell you what's bothering him. Be careful not to probe for details or dwell on the topic. Listen, empathize, and move on. Why? Human nature is funny. Although your customer may be grateful for a friendly ear, in the future he may be uncomfortable with you. He may regret sharing a moment of intimacy with you about something he would rather forget.

If you're dealing with a recurring pattern of bad behavior, it's usually best to address the situation early in the relationship before the situation gets completely out of hand. Let the customer know that you will not tolerate inappropriate behavior.

Let's say the customer has made an off-color joke. You might say something like, "Goodness, you're hurting my ears with that kind of talk. I'm afraid I'll have to go to confession Saturday if I hear another one."

You've used a bit of humor to deflect the offensive behavior, and you've sent a subtle message that lets the customer know you aren't interested in that kind of talk. As always, the key to a good response in a tough situation is to say something consistent with your personality and style.

If the customer doesn't respond to a gentle approach, you may be facing a *serious* problem. There are several alternatives.

1. If the situation allows, speak with the customer privately. Let him know that you cannot tolerate his behavior and explain why. Ask him if he has a problem with you personally. Let him know that his business is very important to you. Give him an opportunity to rectify the situation

2. Ask a colleague to swap this account for another one. Be sure to explain the problem to your colleague first. A different personality changes the dynamics and might result in a better match.

3. If switching isn't feasible, and the private chat doesn't work, speak with the customer's superior about the buyer's behavior. It's risky, but you will probably lose the business anyway if you don't address the issue. It is nearly impossible to maintain a positive business relationship with someone you dislike or don't trust. When speaking with the superior, summarize the steps you've taken to alleviate the problem. Reiterate that their business is very important to you. Ask for help and suggest a solution if you have one.

4. If all else fails, walk away from the business. Let the customer know why.

▶*The customer is always right, but you have rights too.*

Old Tapes

I used to work for an attorney who was also a health care consultant. While driving a particularly long stretch together, he said he was often amused by the stories people told. Most of us, he said, had favorite stories we loved to repeat.

He said you could tell when someone was telling one because it sounded so well practiced and often wasn't entirely relevant to the circumstances. He said, "We play the old tapes in our head just like we do the old cassettes of our favorite music. We play the music because it reminds us of a good time in our past. The same thing happens with our stories."

While storytelling is usually an effective way to make a point, think twice before launching into one of your personal favorites. Discipline yourself to think objectively about the story before you tell it. Ask yourself three questions before telling the story. If the answer to any of these questions is no, save the story for another occasion.

1. Does it really advance the conversation and your goals? Your time in front of the customer is always limited. You can't afford to waste their time with an irrelevant anecdote.
2. Does it reveal something positive about you? It might be a great story but make sure you're not cast as the villain.
3. Will the audience enjoy hearing the story as much as you enjoy telling it? Some of our old favorites are too personal. Sometimes you really did have to be there to appreciate it.

> ▶*Know the difference between old tapes and a story that makes a point.*

Cold Calls

Cold calls are a unique form of sales talk and a wonderful opportunity to practice your sales communication skills. Since cold calls are low risk and they don't take as long as scheduled calls, you can make lots of them.

However, unlike a scheduled appointment, a cold call is an intrusion. You are interrupting someone's schedule, train of thought, or conversation. They have no idea of who you are or what you want. Chances are, you're not even talking to the right person. On the other hand, your prospects get cold calls almost every day. They can spot you the minute your polished shoe shows itself through the office door. They've seen sales-people who are aggressive, those who are cute, and those who are frightened. But most people respond well to people who are confident and poised.

Here are eight communication points that will help you get results from cold calls:

1. *Keep a clear goal in mind.* Before you make the call, have a strong idea of what you want from the call. It might be as simple as getting the decision-maker's name or scheduling an appointment for a later date. You might even expect to make a sale right then and there. Crafting an effective opening sentence or two to get the ball rolling is much easier if you set a specific objective.

2. *Plan your opening.* Your first sentence should be riv-eting. You want to get and then hold your listener's attention. For starters, come up with at least three opening lines. Be creative. Then practice and refine each opening until you're comfortable

3. *Experiment with the openings you develop.* Vary word selection, tone, tempo, and even facial expressions. Try a variety of approaches including humor until you settle on a style that fits your personality and gets results.

4. *Learn to read people's faces.* Are they in a good mood? Do they seem frustrated? Adjust your approach accordingly.

5. *Dress to project the image that best matches the product or service you sell.* What kind of impression do you want to make? For example, would you dress the same way if you were selling financial planning services as you would if you were selling construction materials?

6. *Don't speak until you know you have their full attention.*

When the receptionist asks, "May I help you?" look him or her in the eye, smile, pause a beat, and then speak. Be conversational. You don't want to sound as if you're reading one of your company's marketing brochures.

7. *Speak deliberately.* Resist the temptation to talk too fast to minimize interruption. Going fast in the hope that you'll minimize the interruption helps no one. Remember that your prospects are changing gears, switching from what they were doing to listening to you. Speaking deliberately gives them time to adjust.

8. *Track your progress.* Keep a record of what works and what doesn't. Record what you said, to whom you said it (title, approximate age, sex, time of day, etc.), and the circumstances (i.e., time of day, was the office busy). Keep tracking your progress until you determine what works best for you.

▶*Warm up your cold calls with creative communication.*

Team Selling

Team selling can be a very effective sales technique. In the age of specialization, team selling is increasingly necessary. For one thing, business today is much more focused on technology. We are also forced to operate under complex laws and regulations, including international law. Team selling can give your customer access to a great deal of expertise that you alone simply can't be expected to provide. To get the maximum benefit of a team approach, it is important to understand the communication dynamics and be aware of the pitfalls.

Here are a few key points to remember:

- *Consider whether your expert is a good match with your customer.* Although you may not always have a choice, if you have more than one expert to choose from, do a little match-making. Experts who really connect with your client are worth their weight in gold. Whether it's your finance manager, systems analyst, marketing specialist, or top executive, your first task is coaching your expert on the customer you are visiting. Let your teammates know what you expect of them. Be clear about your objectives and reasons for introducing them to your client. Share any insights you may have about the customer. Failure to adequately prepare your colleagues can put your sale at risk. While there's always a chance that a team member will inadvertently say something that loses the sale, careful planning in advance of your meeting greatly reduces the possibility of disaster.

- *Get the team together ahead of time and compare notes on each presenter's role.* An incredible amount of time is wasted when everyone includes a nearly identical opening remark or graphic meant to tell the customer something about the company. Manage your time effectively. Prepare in advance and coordinate your efforts.

- *Open the meeting by introducing your team members, explaining what they do, and why they are there.* (See the section, "How to Make an Introduction," page 130.) If necessary, provide a brief background of your firm. Next, propose an agenda. You might say, "Mike, I would like to ask Barry to get us started with a demonstration of our service and then have Joanne outline the technical requirements. Is that okay with you?"

- *As each presentation ends, ask for questions while they are fresh in the customer's mind and before you move on to the next speaker.* Multiple presentations are demanding on your audience. Get the audience involved to ensure an exchange of ideas.

- *Make sure you pay strict attention to time limits.* The more people you have, the higher the risk that you will run short of time because each team member will want to make a meaningful contribution. If, for example, you have ninety minutes for four presentations, don't assume that each presenter is entitled to fifteen minutes, leaving thirty minutes for questions. Make sure each team member knows what role you expect them to play and how much time you are giving them.

- *When you structure the meeting, take into account your experts' different communication styles and skills.* For example, if one member of the group is an outstanding, witty performer, while the others are not comfortable with presentations, you probably don't want to put that person on first if you can avoid it. In fact, you may even want that person to facilitate the discussion to take full advantage of her skills without overshadowing others in the group. A facilitator can also keep the meeting moving along and help hold the audience's attention. By the way, if you must follow a particularly strong presenter, and presentations are not one of your strengths, resist the temptation to apologize for your more limited skills. Simply do your very best.

> ▶ *Team selling is an opportunity to deliver your message from a variety of unique viewpoints.*

Making the Most of Trade Shows

You've been assigned to work your company's booth at the annual trade show. It's a demanding assignment. The trade-show floor is the essence of sensory overload: a lot of lights, colors, and exhibits. The hall is crammed with interesting gadgets and sideshows, like magicians, celebrities, and the bright red convertibles that you can win. For the sales professional working the ten-by-ten-foot booth, getting a prospect's attention and holding it long enough to make an impression and an effective presentation is a daunting challenge indeed.

In spite of the distractions, many companies experience terrific sales results at trade shows. In some industries, trade shows are designed for buying, and elaborate exhibits are designed to filter out some of the noise. Perhaps most important, trade shows can be an excellent place to make contacts that lead to sales.

Keep in mind that your products and services are not the only thing on display at one of these shows. Your entire range of communication skills is also on display. Your success in the booth depends on using your skills to maximum effect. Here are fifteen ways you can make the most of the trade show experience:

Sign up as a conference attendee.

Don't just go to the show to work the booth. Sign up as a conference attendee. If your budget permits it, by all means register for the entire show. Some shows include a registration or two for exhibitors. Go to sessions and learn more about what is happening in your industry. Get there a few minutes early so you can meet a few of the other attendees. Network. Invite people to visit your exhibit. Make it a point to ask a good question during the Q&A session. Be sure to identify yourself in the process. Immediately after the session if the presenters are potential prospects, introduce yourself, compliment them on their performance, and exchange business cards.

Make eye contact.

Eye contact and a genuine smile are a very effective way to lure a prospect into your space. Once you've established eye contact, introduce yourself.

Stroll through the exhibits.

What are your competitors emphasizing? Who's exhibiting that might be a customer? Engage their salesperson. Find out who does the buying for them. Collect literature and business cards. When you get back to the office, you'll have some good leads and a head start on your prospect's background.

Stand up.

Never sit down. One CEO I know refuses to permit his sales staff to even have a chair in the booth. There's a good reason for this. If you're sitting down, it might look as though you're taking a break. You're not. You're greeting visitors and showing them your enthusiasm for your products. You're qualifying prospects and building relationships. In the trade show setting, it's hard to do that sitting down.

If you have a large exhibit with a large group representing your company, consider a uniform.

Make it easy for prospects to find you. If your booth is attracting a good crowd, don't make them guess who you are.

Turn off your cell phone!

When I attended a technology conference early last year, I was shocked by how many people supposedly working their booth were engaged in cell phone conversations. We have all been taught not to interrupt someone's conversation. A cell phone has no place on a trade-show floor.

Do not take food or beverages into your booth.

Your booth is not the place to have a snack, sip on a cup of coffee, or chew gum. You are competing with other exhibitors for the attention of convention goers. If you look as though you're taking a break, they'll pass right by you.

Choose your giveaways with care.

While giveaways may seem like a great way to lure people to your booth, they attract everybody, not just legitimate prospects. After working several trade shows, one salesperson I know stopped giving anything away. "This way," she said, "when someone stops by my booth, I know they are a live prospect and not somebody who just wants a multicolored pen." The best giveaway is unique, useful, and has a direct tie-in to your product.

Avoid gimmicks that overshadow your purpose in being at the trade show.

One of my favorites is the magician who gathers a crowd by doing card tricks. The magician cleverly weaves in a few remarks about the company's product, but since he's been hired to put on a show he does so with a wink and nod. Is that really how you want people to perceive your company? Even worse, while the crowd is being entertained, isn't it rude to interrupt your prospects? Then by the time the show is over, they're ready to move on to the next aisle. Do they even remember the company that sponsored the show?

Look at the prospect's business card.

Take a moment to notice their name and what they do before sticking the card in your pocket. It will help you qualify them and often give you a starting point for discussion. Titles are often misleading. If the title is unusual, ask them to explain what they do. Make sure you listen closely to the answer. Don't write on the person's business card. If you need to take notes, do so on a separate piece of paper.

Know your product.

Too often sales representatives are assigned to cover their company's booth before they really know the product. Believe me, it's frustrating to approach a company representative who doesn't know anything more than the basics. When prospects hear, "I just started with the company, let me see if I can find someone to help you," you're imposing on them. Stay out of the exhibit space until you know what you are doing.

Qualify your visitor ASAP.

Are they a prospect? A decision-maker? You certainly don't want to be rude, but you should by all means move along quickly if you are certain that your visitor isn't a prospect. How do you know? Ask them what they do? Ask them if they are familiar with your company and its services. Briefly explain what your firm does and ask them if they can see an application to what they do. With experience you will learn to judge quickly. Just don't be impatient.

Don't even think about the hard sell.

This applies to luring someone into the booth as well as trying to make a sale. Check their body language. If their eyes are swiveling left and right, conclude your pitch and ask if they have any questions. They will appreciate it.

Put a sales team in a room together and they'll talk up a storm for hours.

They catch each other up on their latest deals, the company rumor mill, the family, and that new commission structure. Often good information is exchanged in these forums, but your company's trade show booth is the last place you want to have these discussions. Walk down the aisles of any trade show and you will surely this see this sight over and over again. Three or four people are standing in a tight circle, effectively closing out any prospect who might wander by. Again, we've been taught that it isn't polite to interrupt. So the prospect walks buy, glancing at the exhibit and making a mental note to stop by again later. Only a few will actually circle back. The rest are gone. The temptation to participate in these conversations can be overwhelming. But what message are you sending about your company? What does it say about you? That closed circle communicates that you are not open for business. It says, "Go away, I'm busy."

Keep your competitors out of your booth.

Friendly competition is fine, but this is no time to be exchanging stories or sharing information that a competitor can use against you. Body language alone is usually sufficient to discourage such visits.

▶*Trade shows are an expensive investment.*
Get your money's worth.

Negotiating

Successful negotiation requires skill and experience. Most of us like to think we are good negotiators, but there is a world of difference between negotiating a good price on a new car and negotiating with a customer you will be serving in the future. Transactions like buying a car or a new TV are arm's length, short-term relationships. Negotiating with a customer is much more complicated because in most situations you cannot use the negotiating techniques that, say, a labor negotiator might use. Why? Once the bargaining is over, you must revert back to the role of the customer's friend, consultant, and even confidant. If you insist on putting on your tough, gun-slinging negotiator hat to get an agreement, don't expect your customer to respond with warmth just because you switched back to your sales professional cap as soon as the deal is struck. It pays to remember that after the agreement is signed, you will still have a relationship with your customer.

Even if you enjoyed an excellent relationship with the client before negotiating, you run the risk of damaging, if not destroying, the relationship unless you continue to make the relationship a priority through the negotiation process.

Whatever your bargaining strategy is, take the time necessary to plan the way you will communicate your position. For example, when you've made all the concessions you can make, avoid backing yourself or the customer into a corner. Saying "this is my final offer" or "take it or leave it" can get you in hot water quickly. If you plan ahead for this moment, you'll be more likely to express yourself in a nonconfrontational manner. You might say, "I need your help here. I can't do any better than what I've offered in this area." Make your point without sounding as though you're issuing a threat. If you reach an end point without having a communication strategy, you're more likely to use blunt terms, especially if negotiations have been difficult. Not only do harsh words make it more difficult to get an agreement, they can spoil the relationship as well.

Recognize that the bargaining position itself can communicate a great deal about you and your company. A former associate told me a story that illustrates this point. He was involved in negotiation with a key vendor. They had a long-standing exclusive business relationship. Sometimes, he even socialized with the vendor. When it came time to renew the agreement, the vendor surprised my friend with a request for a 25 percent increase in fees. Historically, the fees had increased at a rate of less than 5 percent annually. The existing agreement had a clause that gave the customer the right to review the vendor's books.

Rather than take such a drastic measure, the customer did some calculating based on what he knew about the vendor's business. He was shocked to discover that in all likelihood, the vendor's annual profit already exceeded 60 percent of the fees he was currently paying. The customer asked repeatedly for an explanation of the need for the 25 percent increase but couldn't seem to pin down the vendor to anything specific. Finally, out of frustration the customer countered with an offer to reduce the *current* fees.

The vendor was shocked. He complained loudly. He continued to offer vague reasons for needing the increase. The customer, sensing that something was not right, held firm. Cornered, the vendor finally asked, sheepish grin on his face, "Can't I at least get a little increase? Is your offer really a decrease?" They settled on a 2 percent increase. But my friend told me he started looking for another vendor immediately. A year later he switched vendors in spite of the fact that service levels had remained top notch. He said, "I just didn't trust the guy anymore."

It's okay to be a tough negotiator, but you must bend over backward to be honest and fair. Remember, you're not a free agent negotiating a contract for your client. You're trying to develop a new relationship or strengthen an existing one. If you've positioned yourself as a consultative sales professional, for example, you may find it extremely hard to recapture that position in the customer's mind if your bargaining posture is winner takes all. Keep that in mind when it's time to negotiate a new agreement.

Legitimate disagreements frequently arise in the course of negotiating an agreement. When it happens, focus your communication skills harder than ever on listening to the customer's point of view. Make sure you really understand their position. Ask probing questions. Try to put yourself in their shoes.

Restate their position, over and over again if necessary, until you have their agreement that you have stated it accurately. If you take the time to understand their position, see it from their viewpoint, you'll increase your chances of finding a workable solution.

As I said at the outset, negotiation requires skill and experience. The best sales professionals learn the art and science of negotiating. By developing strong communication skills, you will improve your ability to negotiate successfully. There are some excellent books on negotiation that will help you become a better negotiator. I've referenced one of them in the recommended reading section of the book.

▶ *Successful negotiation requires clear thinking, plain speech, and active listening.*

Sales Talk in Your Office

As a former colleague put it, "A lot of sales are killed before the salesperson ever leaves the office." What is the environment around your office? What do you and your colleagues talk about when the boss is not around? What role do you play in making the office environment what it is? Are you enthusiastic about your company and its products? Or do you tend to find fault with the way things are done? Do you encourage your coworkers to do their best, sharing new ideas with them? Or are you so competitive you take every opportunity to cut them down to size?

Whatever your attitude is around the office, it will almost certainly carry over into your sales calls. You can't afford negative thoughts or feelings. Verbalizing them on a regular basis will hurt your performance. No doubt there will always be sales representatives who are unhappy about something. Whether it's the commission plan, their territory, or the sales manager they don't like, there is always something. When it's isolated, it isn't a serious problem.

But negative attitudes, if not isolated, can spread like a flu virus with the same deleterious results. While you can't completely avoid hearing negative talk, you don't have to participate in it. Limit your role to being a good listener. If it's appropriate to the circumstances, make constructive suggestions. Make sure that your own attitude is upbeat. Lead by example. Be the one who is always looking for the silver lining, ready to attack problems until they are solved. Be the first to congratulate someone else's success. Be there to encourage them when they trip. Don't feel as though you have to be a cheerleader if that isn't your style. You can achieve the same results quietly if it suits you.

If your office is a breeding ground for negative communication, do what you can to change the environment. If you can't influence positive changes in the environment, decide whether this is the right organization for you. A positive attitude is integral to your success. A firm that doesn't provide a good environment is a sinking ship.

Communicating a positive attitude around the office isn't limited to the sales staff. Demonstrate the same upbeat persona to everyone you interact with in your company. When a sales professional has a good attitude, it gives everyone a needed lift. If you're feeling good, sales must be going through the roof. Maybe a big order is just about to come through. If your positive attitude helps people feel good about their work, they'll perform better for your customers.

Take the time to meet and get to know key people in your organization. Let them know what you're working on. Keep them up-to-date on what customers are saying about the quality of your company's service. There are significant benefits to spending time with the accountants, the men and women on the assembly line, the warehouse staff, the marketing group, and so on. Rarely if ever do these folks get to see firsthand how customers benefit from their efforts. They will appreciate that you took the time to make it real for them. Eventually, you will need their help with something. Are they more likely to respond if you have taken the time to communicate with them when you didn't need something? You bet. Treat all coworkers as customers, too.

▶*When you're in the office, make it your business
to charge everyone's battery.*

Selling Technology

Buying technology driven products and services can be a trying experience. From buying a sound system to a personal computer to a software solution, the experience is much the same. Either the sales representative seems to know way more than you do but can't explain it in terms you understand, or knows even less than you do but is hoping you won't notice.

If you are selling technology, here are ten rules to help you make the experience pleasant for your customer:

1. *Encourage your customers to ask questions.* Many people fear technology as a result of negative past experiences. They don't know the lingo and may be afraid of looking ignorant or even foolish. They are worried that they will make a mistake that costs the company a lot of time and money. Gently probe to understand their concerns and then deal with them head-on. Your customers will appreciate it.

2. *Learn the language.* If you're selling a Web-based service, for example, you don't need to know the details of what makes it work. But you should be able to answer general questions about programming language, security protocols, and the various reports without hesitation or fumbling. Know the technical terms and be prepared to explain them in simple terms.

3. *Don't use acronyms.* ERP stands for enterprise resource planning. You know the term, but does your customer? It's easy to slip into this kind of talk, especially if you use it around the office every day. Stay away from the acronyms until you are sure your customer is on your level.

4. *Don't assume your customers understand what you are talking about.* Ask them if you are making yourself clear. If it's feasible, bring the product with you. Put it in their hands and let them try it out.

5. *Humanize the technology.* When I was selling Web-based health care transactions, our target market was the business office staff in hospitals and doctor's offices. Many of our prospects were not computer literate. One of our account executives became a big favorite when it

came time to demonstrate our service because she was able to relate the technology on the screen to everyday occurrences. For example, the cursor, shaped like an arrow, became the "mommy finger." When the well-known hourglass flipped up and down, she simply said, "The computer is thinking." She was a big hit.

6. *If you don't know the answer to something, say so.* Never try to fake it. While it might appear as if no one in the audience knows very much about technology, sometimes people deliberately hold back, waiting to see how much you know. Bluffing will kill your sale every time. Get back to them when you know the answer.

7. *If you are selling to technical people and the discussion becomes too technical for you, don't be afraid to ask questions.* For one thing, you need to be sure they are not off on a tangent. You might also learn something new. On the other hand, if technical talk goes over your head too often, consider a team selling approach. Bring your in-house expert along with you until you get comfortable with the language.

8. *Don't fall in love with your technology.* Too often, I've seen sales professionals get so wrapped up in the technology that they have forgotten the customer. Don't dwell on product features just because you find the technology compelling. You might love it, but does it do anything for the client?

9. *Consider carefully whether every feature of your product is really a benefit to your customer.* Just because it exists doesn't mean you have to talk about it. Too many features confuse people. Keep it simple, moving on to new features only when you are sure your customer is comfortable with what you've discussed so far.

10. *Include a glossary of technical terms in your marketing*

materials and proposals. Your prospects will appreciate the opportunity to familiarize themselves with key terms.

▶*Get comfortable selling technology.*
It isn't going away.

Breaking Bread

The business meal is a time-honored tradition. Sales professionals use business meals to build rapport with the customer, move a sale along, or celebrate the closing of a new deal. Having a meal with your customer has obvious advantages. Entertainment creates good will. The setting is often more intimate. You're on neutral turf. Frequently, you can improve your chances of achieving your purpose by meeting away from the distractions of an office environment.

Of course, there are a few downsides. For one thing, there is the risk of becoming too familiar. The temptation to say something you wouldn't think of saying in an office setting is always there. Also, if you have a serious issue to resolve, a restaurant with the noise, hustle and bustle, and interruptions can make it exceedingly hard to accomplish anything. You need a communication strategy to help you get the most out of these events.

Most business meals have a few common elements:

- A period of small talk
- The ordering ritual
- Serving/eating
- Dessert/coffee
- Business discussion

Some sales professionals will initiate a discussion during or between these segments. For example, waiting for the meal to arrive, the salesperson may say, "Maybe we can cover a few items before the food gets here . . . "

Invariably, just as the conversation is making progress, the server interrupts, serving meals along with happy talk, which interrupts your momentum. It also tends to result in conversation that bounces back and forth between business discussion and socializing. This isn't necessarily a bad thing, but it can play havoc with your momentum.

When should you initiate the business discussion? Keep in mind that business meals impose time limits. Typically, you have no more than an hour for breakfast, an hour and a half for lunch, and maybe two hours for dinner. Whether you can accomplish your objective in the time available is an important consideration when deciding between a breakfast, lunch, or dinner appointment.

Since a breakfast meeting is usually brief, it's not impolite to begin discussing business immediately after exchanging pleasantries. Let the setting determine when to initiate discussion at lunch. In an informal atmosphere like a luncheonette, you can begin soon after you're seated. If it's a more formal setting, wait until you've ordered and the small talk has subsided.

Strapped for time, most business people today won't linger over coffee at lunch. At dinner meetings though, it's polite to hold business discussions until the coffee is served. Dinners tend to be more social than other meals. They occur after-hours when your client has already had a full day.

Other Considerations
- *Be sure to think about what restaurant selection communicates to the customer.* Dinner in a five star restaurant certainly communicates something different than breakfast at the local diner. Let the situation dictate your choice; remember there is a fine line between entertainment and manipulation.

- *Take the time to communicate expectations about the purpose of the meeting.* Be specific about your intentions and what you hope to accomplish. Be just as clear about the type of dining experience you are proposing. If you say, "I would like to take you to lunch next week. If you're available let's meet in your lobby at noon," it would be natural for the customer to assume you are taking them to a restaurant. Taking them across the street for a hot dog from the street vendor could be a letdown indeed, unless you make your intentions known in advance. Then you could say, "Bob, I'm going to be in your area tomorrow, I have a tight schedule, but could I interest you in a quick hot dog so I can drop off those figures you requested?"
- *Keep it light.* Try to focus the conversation on one significant topic. That's enough for a meal.
- *Liquor and business rarely make a good combination.* While a cocktail before, and a glass of wine during dinner is certainly acceptable, drinking in moderation is always advisable. Go easy on alcoholic refreshments, for your sake and your client's.
- *Be a gracious and generous host.* Work hard to make your guests feel welcome and comfortable. Pay special attention to anyone who seems shy, even if they are not the key decision-makers. Earn their support too. Aside from the fact that it's your responsibility to engage everyone, the quiet ones probably have more influence than you realize.

▶ *A business meal is in itself a form of communication.*
Plan accordingly.

Gifts

Gift giving is an act of communication. While extravagance is not necessary, thoughtfulness and consideration are. Spending too much may insult your client's integrity. On the other hand, giving them a T-shirt featuring your company's logo isn't a truly thoughtful gesture, because the buyer is well aware that you have cases of them sitting in your warehouse in all sizes.

Why not make an extra effort to personalize your gifts? Let's say that your customer, who lives in Seattle, mentions that she just loves *Freihofer* cookies, produced by a regional bakery located in New York. When your travels take you to Albany, pick up a couple of boxes and ship them to the client. You didn't spend a lot of money, but believe me, your customer will remember it. After all, mentioning the cookies was probably just an off-hand remark that wasn't even supposed to register with you. That you heard and acted upon it sends a strong message about your thoughtfulness, command of details, and follow-through.

Giving gifts to valued customers during the holidays is another time-honored tradition. Having been the recipient of holiday-related gifts, I certainly appreciate them, but I can't help wondering whether they are practical from a business perspective. For one thing, customers tend to get lots of gifts during the holidays. In the health care industry, it's usually something edible. Once or twice a day, a box appears in my office. Frankly, it's hard to keep track. Also, holiday gifts are not usually given with an individual in mind, making them impersonal. Pay attention to what really turns your customers on. When the holidays arrive, you can really knock their socks off with a gift that's truly personalized. Believe me, they will remember it.

> ▶*If you must give your customer a gift, take the time to make it memorable.*

Humor

Humor is a versatile communication tool. You'll notice that effective speechmakers often begin their speeches with humor to break the ice, connect with the audience, and set a positive listening tone. In sales, a humorous opening is a great way to get your customer's attention. Remember, being witty doesn't always have to get a belly laugh. A self-deprecating remark that gets a genuine smile is enough.

Humor can also be an effective device to diffuse tension. I remember arriving late for a project meeting with several colleagues. What made it worse was that it was the third time I was late for the weekly meeting. The look on my colleagues' faces left no doubt. They were seething. I didn't say a word. I sat down, opened my briefcase, and pulled out a deck of tarot cards that a friend had given me the day before. With a completely straight face, I displayed the cards on the table and said, "Who wants to go first?" It broke up the room. I then quickly made my excuses and we got on with the meeting.

Some people are naturally funny, with a well-developed sense of humor and a knack for timing. It's a wonderful gift. If you've been blessed with that particular talent, by all means take advantage of it.

If humor doesn't come naturally to you, don't sweat it. You may not deliver many great lines, but you can have a good sense of humor, including the ability to laugh at yourself. You can also improve your ability to be funny by studying comedy. What makes you laugh? Why is it funny? Pay special attention to the way humor is delivered. Is there a pause at the right moment that sets up the laugh line? Learn to look for the humor in everyday life. There's certainly enough to go around. Remember too that humor that derives from the situation is often the most effective form of comedy. Jokes, on the other hand, tend to beget jokes and precious time with your client can be wasted.

While humor is a very effective ally, handle it with care using these tips.

- Don't overdo it. You're not developing a stand-up routine. Humor is a tool, but it shouldn't overshadow you or your product.

- If your funny story falls flat, just go on with the business at hand. Don't fret over it and don't chastise your audience for not getting the joke. Maybe your timing was off. Learn from your mistakes. In a sales situation, usually the best humor is the kind you turn inward, meaning the joke is on you.
- Avoid humor that relies on sexual references or belittling ethnic background, race, religion, or disabilities. There are no exceptions.
- Humor at someone else's expense, especially the customer's, is almost always a mistake—even if you feel you've gotten to know the client well.

I once made a minor connection with a sales representative from a medical supplies distributor over the fact that his wife, like me, was an Italian American from New Jersey.

He took that little opening too far in our next meeting. He mentioned that his wife's uncle, Joe D, called and said he would be in town and wanted to visit them in their Minneapolis home. Then he said, significantly, "He's in the *Family*, so I wasn't about to say no." For the record, there was no mistaking his meaning.

Now I am not usually offended by such remarks. But I was offended by his comment. It was presumptuous, implying that we shared an intimate friendship when we barely knew each other.

We certainly were not close enough for him to take that particular liberty. I wasn't even a customer yet. His remark reduced his prospects for a sale. Not consciously perhaps, but his comment was a turnoff. There were, of course, several good business reasons to choose another supplier. Then again, at what point did I stop listening?

"A jest often decides matters of importance more effectually and happily than seriousness."

—Horace

Chapter 11

A Few Final Thoughts

Now that you've reached the final chapter, I hope you can see what I saw as I wrote this book—a lot of communication is common sense. Although you don't have to have a Harvard MBA to communicate, you do have to be a keen observer of people. You must have a genuine interest in reaching your audience.

Perhaps the most interesting thing about communication is that no matter how much you learn, regardless of how effective you become, there is always more to learn and room for improvement. Don't be discouraged when you slip up and say the wrong thing. Even the most experienced communicators make mistakes. Learn from these experiences. Your goal is not perfection—it's steady improvement.

As I wrote this book and I met with sales professionals on a regular basis, I became much more aware of communication styles and differences in ability. I am convinced more than ever that the ability to communicate effectively is the number one skill you must have to succeed in sales.

As you improve your communication skills, let your confidence show in your words, your voice, your gestures, your body language, and eye contact. When you make a sales call, you have only a few minutes to make a lasting impression. Prepare for every call, making certain that your preparation includes a carefully planned communication strategy.

By improving your communication skills, you will make more sales. With a passion for your product, persistence, and the ability to effectively deliver your message, your success is guaranteed.

Finally, I would love to hear from you. If you have any questions or comments about *Sales Talk* you can e-mail me at *lenms@salestalk.biz.*

"I'll pay more for the ability to speak than for any other quality a person might possess."

—Charles Schwab

Recommended
Reading

Researching *Sales Talk* was a pleasure. I discovered (in some cases, rediscovered) some terrific books on selling and communication skills. Here is a baker's dozen that I recommend highly.

Ailes, Roger. *You Are the Messenger.* New York: Doubleday/Currency, 1988.

Beckwith, Harry. *Selling the Invisible.* New York: Warner Books, 1997.

———. *The Invisible Touch.* New York: Warner Books, 2000.

Elster, Charles Harrington. *The Verbal Advantage.* New York: Random House, 2000.

Hoff, Ron. *I Can See You Naked.* Kansas City: Andrews and McMeel, 1992.

McCormack, Mark H. *On Selling.* West Hollywood, CA: Dove Books, 1996.

Pachter, Barbara. *When the Little Things Count.* New York: Marlowe & Co., 2001.

Rackham, Neil. *The Spin Selling Fieldbook.* New York: McGraw Hill, 1996.

Richardson, Linda. *Stop Telling Start Selling.* New York: McGraw Hill, 1998.

Ries, Al and Jack Trout. *The 22 Immutable Laws of Marketing.* New York: Harper Business, 1993.

Ruben, Brent and Lea P. Stewart. *Communication and Human Behavior.* Needham Heights, MA: Allyn and Bacon, 1998.

Shell, G. Richard. *Bargaining for Advantage.* New York: Penguin Putnam, Inc., 1999.

Sjodin, Terri L. *New Sales Speak.* New York: John Wiley & Sons, Inc., 2001.

Index

A

B

C

STREETWISE® BOOKS

New Releases!

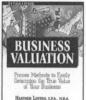

Adams *Streetwise*® books for growing your business

About the Author

Len Serafino spent ten successful years selling medical equipment and services to doctors, hospitals, and HMOs, and has taught selling skills to hundreds of people. He has also spent many years as a buyer of health care services. Having sat on both sides of the table, he brings a unique perspective to the art and science of selling. His articles have appeared in *Toastmaster Magazine* and *HomeCare Magazine*.